Test Your Rock IQ
THE '60s

Also by Ira Robbins

The Trouser Press Record Guide
The Rolling Stone Review 1985
Test Your Rock IQ: The '70s

Test Your Rock IQ
THE '60s

....

250 Mindbenders
from Rock's Glory Decade

Ira Robbins

Illustrations by Nick DeBenedetto

Little, Brown and Company
Boston - New York - Toronto - London

First Edition

Library of Congress Cataloging-in-Publication Data

Robbins, Ira A.
   Test your rock IQ: the '60s: folk rock and acid rock, bubblegum and Woodstock, 250 mindbenders from rock's glory decade / Ira Robbins: illustrations by Nick DeBenedetto.–1st ed.
       p. cm.
   ISBN 0-316-74898-6
   1. Rock music–1961–1970–Miscellanea. I. Title. II. Title:
'60s.
ML3534.R55 1993
781.66'09–dc20   93-13673

10 9 8 7 6 5 4 3 2 1

Book design by Martha Kennedy

RRD-VA

Published simultaneously in Canada by Little, Brown & Company (Canada) Limited

Printed in the United States of America

ACKNOWLEDGMENTS

My thanks go to everyone who helped: my editor and friend Michael Pietsch for coming up with this project and for getting me into books in the first place; Wayne King, Dave Schulps, Jim Green, and Scott Schinder for their scholarship and suggestions. I am indebted to my buddy Nick DeBenedetto for meeting an art-in-a-hurry deadline with flying pen strokes. My love goes to Mom and Dad and Bobo for the usual stuff.

Ira Robbins
New York City

Test Your Rock IQ
THE '60s

Introduction

For a 12-year-old in New York City in 1966, there were three crucial choices that had to be made if life was going to proceed: Yankees or Mets, Rolling Stones or Beatles, and WMCA or WABC. Me, I had no problem picking the Bronx Bombers and the WMCA Good Guys, but musical allegiances were much harder to pin down. It wasn't simply deciding that Mick was a better singer than Paul or that "19th Nervous Breakdown" was deeper than "Paperback Writer." (For songs that meant something, it was always Bob Dylan by a landslide.) The problem was there was just too damn much wonderful music blaring from my 17-transistor Viscount radio to rule any out.

Here's the top 10 of WMCA's Radio 57 countdown survey for the week of April 28, 1966:

1. Mamas and Papas: "Monday Monday"
2. Young Rascals: "Good Lovin'"
3. Righteous Brothers: "(You're My) Soul and Inspiration"
4. Beach Boys: "Sloop John B"
5. Cher: "Bang Bang (My Baby Shot Me Down)"
6. Percy Sledge: "When a Man Loves a Woman"
7. Outsiders: "Time Won't Let Me"
8. Paul Revere and the Raiders: "Kicks"
9. Johnny Rivers: "Secret Agent Man"
10. Bob Dylan: "Rainy Day Women #12 and 35"

Okay, maybe the Cher song is a melodramatic howler, but that's nine truly classic songs out of ten. Songs that have endured by groups that, except for the Outsiders, really mattered in some historical sense.

And the rest of the chart is filled with equally eclectic greats: Louis Armstrong, James Brown, Kinks, Hollies, Byrds, Supremes, Frank Sinatra, Simon and Garfunkel, the Lovin' Spoonful. What made the decade's music so special was its unpredictability. Nothing was forbidden, and the oddest things–from a Green Beret defending war to a hippie singing about peace, a soul man

championing black pride to a stupid novelty record about insanity–were all accepted into the pop mainstream.

For some of us, rock 'n' roll was the key to growing up. I learned about love, sex, politics, language, and geography from records. I built friendships around groups, marked my life with songs, and discovered that a jukebox in Switzerland could carry me home on a guitar solo. And through it all, bits and pieces of knowledge stuck in my head, filling up a mental attic with useless information about long-disbanded groups and records I haven't played in two decades.

Rock trivia isn't a nerdy hobby like matchbook collecting, it's a scrapbook of memories with a beat. The names and dates and labels matter only in terms of the music they brought us. So I hope this book is taken in the spirit with which it's intended: less a yardstick than an entertaining reminder of what you know about the sounds of the '60s and an introduction to some of what you don't. If this book inspires you to go back and play some records you forgot you had, that's what it's all about.

Scoring

There are five quizzes of increasing difficulty in this book. Each quiz contains 50 questions. The answers have points indicated, so if you want to grade your expertise or challenge your friends to a rock trivia showdown, number a sheet of paper 1 to 50 and write down your answers. At the end of the quiz, compare your answers to those in the answer section at the back of the book and tote up your score. A perfect score for each quiz is 500.

In the interests of a chronologically level playing field, younger players should be given a handicap—say, 10 points per year born after 1960. After all, it's a lot easier to remember this stuff if you lived through it.

Ratings

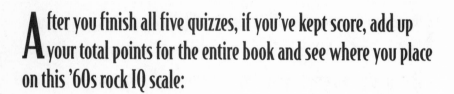

After you finish all five quizzes, if you've kept score, add up your total points for the entire book and see where you place on this '60s rock IQ scale:

under 500:	Dropout from the college of musical knowledge
500–1000:	One-hit wonder
1001–1500:	Keep a knockin'
1501–2000:	Vinyl junkie
2001–2500:	Have you ever considered writing rock quiz books?

QUIZ 1:

EASY TO BE HARD

Let's get started with this elementary warm-up: multiple choices and match games concerning band names, song and album titles, and a bit of rock history about the Beatles, Rolling Stones, and other memorable stars of the '60s. So get out your 45 spindle and those old issues of <u>Hit Parader</u> and see how much you can remember.

'60S ROCK HISTORY 101

1. At the Beatles' Royal Command Performance in London, November 1963, which one of the Fab Four had the cheek to request that "the people in the cheaper seats clap your hands, and the rest of you, if you'd just rattle your jewelry"?

   (a) John Lennon
   (b) Paul McCartney
   (c) George Harrison
   (d) Ringo Starr
   (e) Pete Best

2. In July 1966, a catastrophe nearly ended Bob Dylan's career. What happened?

   (a) onstage electrocution
   (b) drug overdose
   (c) tax audit
   (d) motorcycle crash
   (e) food poisoning

3. Which singer was arrested in Miami on March 1, 1969, for allegedly exposing himself onstage?

   (a) Bo Diddley
   (b) Mick Jagger
   (c) Jim Morrison
   (d) Little Richard
   (e) Janis Joplin

4. In April 1968, the first rock musical opened on Broadway. It was later made into a film. Which one was it?

   (a) Tommy
   (b) Godspell
   (c) Hair
   (d) Jesus Christ Superstar

(e) <u>You're a Good Man, Charlie Brown</u>

5. In late 1965, a concert promoter opened the soon-to-be-legendary Fillmore Auditorium in San Francisco with a bill featuring the Jefferson Airplane. Who was this great rock 'n' roll impresario?

(a) David Peel
(b) Alan Freed
(c) Sid Bernstein
(d) Jerry Garcia
(e) Bill Graham

THE NAME GAME

6. Put these 10 songs in ascending order by the numbers that belong where the "X" in their titles is:

(a) "If X Was 9" (Jimi Hendrix Experience)
(b) "Cloud X" (Temptations)
(c) "Five to X" (Doors)
(d) "Quarter to X" (Gary U.S. Bonds)
(e) "X and 7 Is" (Love)
(f) "X Miles High" (Byrds)
(g) "Let the X Winds Blow" (Fats Domino)
(h) "X Lovers" (Mary Wells)
(i) "X Little Indians" (Yardbirds)
(j) "X O'Clock World" (Vogues)

7. Using the list provided, fill in the animals—mundane and exotic—missing from these '60s song titles:

Rabbit	Albatross
Cats	Tiger
Rat	Rooster
Dog	Kangaroo
Monkey	Flamingo

(a) "White _____" (Jefferson Airplane)
(b) "Nashville _____" (Lovin' Spoonful)
(c) "Tie Me _____Down, Sport" (Rolf Harris)
(d) "Pressed _____and Warthog" (Cream)
(e) "I've Got a _____by the Tail" (Buck Owens)
(f) "A Salty _____" (Procol Harum)
(g) "Little Red _____" (Rolling Stones)
(h) "Pretty _____" (Manfred Mann)
(i) "_____" (Fleetwood Mac)
(j) "Mickey's _____" (Miracles)

8. From this collection of comestibles, fill in the missing edible from these '60s group names:

Chocolate	Lemon	Grape
Jelly	Spinach	Strawberry
Fruitgum	Peanut Butter	Prunes
Fudge		

(a) _____Alarm Clock
(b) Ultimate _____
(c) _____Pipers
(d) Vanilla _____
(e) _____Conspiracy
(f) _____Watch Band
(g) Electric _____
(h) 1910 _____Company
(i) Moby _____
(j) Heavy _____

9. Disregarding anything Funk and Wagnalls may have to say, exactly how did these bands (mis)spell their names?

(a) Vanity Fair
(b) Tea Set
(c) Circle

(d) Frigid Pink
(e) Spiral Staircase

10. Elvis Presley will always be the King, but other artists have earned enduring epithets as well. Who are

(a) The Godfather of Soul
(b) The Killer
(c) The King of the Blues
(d) The Queen of Soul
(e) God

MATCHES

11. Match up these lead singers and their groups:

(a) Eric Burdon	Herman's Hermits
(b) Burton Cummings	Paul Revere and the Raiders
(c) John Fogerty	Blood, Sweat and Tears
(d) Mark Lindsay	Lovin' Spoonful
(e) Curtis Mayfield	Guess Who
(f) Peter Noone	Animals
(g) Reg Presley	Impressions
(h) Keith Relf	Creedence Clearwater Revival
(i) John Sebastian	Troggs
(j) David Clayton-Thomas	Yardbirds

12. Match up these Somebody and the Somethings:

(a) Freddie	Family Stone
(b) Tommy James	Pacemakers
(c) Smokey Robinson	Blue Belles
(d) Martha	Mindbenders
(e) Gerry	Union Gap

(f)	Sly	Shondells
(g)	Wayne Fontana	Detroit Wheels
(h)	Gary Puckett	Dreamers
(i)	Patti LaBelle	Miracles
(j)	Mitch Ryder	Vandellas

13. Match up these singing duos:

(a)	Chad	Gordon
(b)	Ike	Jeremy
(c)	Jan	Tina
(d)	Peter	Dave
(e)	Sam	Dean

14. Match up these one-hit wonders and their lone Top 40 hits:

(a)	Blues Magoos	"Judy in Disguise (with Glasses)"
(b)	Count Five	"Come on Down to My Boat"
(c)	Every Mothers' Son	"Eve of Destruction"
(d)	John Fred and His	"Dirty Water"
	Playboy Band	"Classical Gas"
(e)	Richard Harris	"Psychotic Reaction"
(f)	Hombres	"Elusive Butterfly"
(g)	Bob Lind	"(We Ain't Got) Nothin' Yet"
(h)	Barry McGuire	"Let It Out (Let It All Hang Out)"
(i)	Standells	"MacArthur Park"
(j)	Mason Williams	

15. Match up the album and the artist who made it:

(a)	Days of Future Passed	Cream
(b)	Electric Ladyland	Jefferson Airplane
(c)	Everybody's in Show-Biz	Mothers of Invention
(d)	John Wesley Harding	Jimi Hendrix Experience

(e) I Got Dem Ol' Kozmic   Creedence Clearwater Revival
    Blues Again, Mama   Moody Blues
(f) Stand!   Janis Joplin
(g) Surrealistic Pillow   Kinks
(h) We're Only in It   Bob Dylan
    for the Money   Sly and the Family Stone
(i) Wheels of Fire
(j) Willy and the Poor Boys

BEATLES, ROLLING STONES, KINKS, OR THE WHO

16. Which one of the four British groups did these songs?

(a) "She's a Woman"
(b) "She's a Rainbow"
(c) "She's Got Everything"
(d) "It's a Boy"
(e) "I'm a Boy"
(f) "Boys"
(g) "Wonderboy"
(h) "In Another Land"
(i) "Rael"
(j) "Shangri La"

HITS OR MISSES

17. Of these ten '60s classics, only five actually made Billboard's Top 40 album charts. The rest got the glory without the accompanying sales figures. Which five met with commercial success?

(a) Magic Bus: The Who on Tour
(b) The Velvet Underground & Nico

(c) Another Side of Bob Dylan
(d) Cream: Disraeli Gears
(e) Byrds: Sweetheart of the Rodeo
(f) Bob Dylan: Highway 61 Revisited
(g) Kinks-Size
(h) Joni Mitchell: Clouds
(i) Pink Floyd: Ummagumma
(j) The Who Sell Out

SUPREMES, SHANGRI-LAS, SHIRELLES, OR THE RONETTES

18. Which of the four great girl groups did these unforgettable songs?

(a) "Baby Love"
(b) "Be My Baby"
(c) "Baby It's You"
(d) "Baby, I Love You"
(e) "Remember (Walkin' in the Sand)"
(f) "Walking in the Rain"
(g) "Dedicated to the One I Love"
(h) "Where Did Our Love Go"
(i) "Will You Love Me Tomorrow?"
(j) "Love Is Like an Itching in My Heart"

AMERICAN OR BRITISH

19. Give these artists their correct nationality.

(a) Cyrkle
(b) Hollies
(c) Left Banke
(d) Keith

(e) Blues Magoos
(f) Petula Clark
(g) Dusty Springfield
(h) Beau Brummels
(i) Procol Harum
(j) Association

DYLAN, DONOVAN, PHIL OCHS, OR THE LOVIN' SPOONFUL

20. Match up these folk and folk-rock songs with the artists who wrote and/or sang them.

(a) "Darling Be Home Soon"
(b) "Colours"
(c) "Tape from California"
(d) "To Susan on the West Coast Waiting"
(e) "Catch the Wind"
(f) "Flower Lady"
(g) "Sad-Eyed Lady of the Lowlands"
(h) "Do You Believe in Magic"
(i) "Ballad of Oxford (Jimmy Meredith)"
(j) "Oxford Town"

ROCKIN' ALL OVER THE GLOBE

21. To which city did Dionne Warwick request directions in her 1968 hit?

(a) Santa Fe
(b) San Jose
(c) East L.A.
(d) Allentown, PA
(e) Boise

22. With the Beatles' "A Day in the Life" in mind, what English county contains the city of Blackburn?

    (a) Worcestershire
    (b) Lancashire
    (c) Gloucestershire
    (d) Westminster
    (e) Essex

23. In what city is the "House of the Rising Sun"?

    (a) Tokyo
    (b) Chicago
    (c) Memphis
    (d) New York
    (e) New Orleans

24. Where did the Beatles play their final concert on August 29, 1966?

    (a) San Francisco
    (b) New York
    (c) Liverpool
    (d) London
    (e) Chicago

25. Match the song titles and the place names missing from them:

(a) "_____Stomp" (Dovells, 1961)	New York City
(b) "_____Lulu" (Jan and Dean, 1963)	Waterloo
(c) "_____Sun" (Rivieras, 1964)	England
(d) "Girl from_____" (Stan Getz/Astrud Gilberto, 1964)	California
	Phoenix
(e) "The Boy from _____" (Ad-Libs, 1965)	Kentucky
(f) "_____Swings" (Roger Miller, 1965)	New York
(g) "_____Woman" (Neil Diamond, 1967)	Bristol
(h) "_____Mining Disaster" (Bee Gees, 1967)	Ipanema
(i) "By the Time I Get to_____" (Glen Campbell, 1967)	Honolulu

(j) "_____Sunset" (Kinks, 1967)

'60S ROCK HISTORY 102

26. Which legendary Mississippi blues guitarist and singer of the 1930s provided significant inspiration (and such songs as "Crossroads" and "Love in Vain") for both Cream and the Rolling Stones?

(a) Sonny Boy Williamson
(b) John Lee Hooker
(c) Willie Dixon
(d) Robert Johnson
(e) Blind Lemon Jefferson

27. Which 1965 song, originally recorded by an acoustic folk duo that had already broken up, was electrified in the studio without the artists' knowledge and became a chart-topping folk-rock hit?

(a) "Do You Believe in Magic" (Lovin' Spoonful)
(b) "When Will I Be Loved" (Everly Brothers)
(c) "I Got You Babe" (Sonny and Cher)
(d) "Pushin' Too Hard" (Seeds)
(e) "Sounds of Silence" (Simon and Garfunkel)

28. What American singer reached the top of the singles charts only after his death in 1967, when a song that he had recorded in his last week alive was posthumously released?

(a) Eddie Cochran
(b) Otis Redding
(c) Gene Vincent
(d) Bobby Darin
(e) Sam Cooke

29. What British art-rock group was banned from London's Royal Albert Hall after burning an American flag onstage during a 1968 performance of a piece from <u>West Side Story</u>?

    (a) Roxy Music

    (b) Yes

    (c) Nektar

    (d) Nice

    (e) King Crimson

30. Upon recording Paul McCartney's "Come and Get It" for Apple Records in 1969, a British group called the Iveys rechristened itself and became a Top 10 act in England and America. Under what name did the band become famous?

    (a) Hot Chocolate

    (b) Bonzo Dog Doo-Dah Band

    (c) Babys

    (d) Crickets

    (e) Badfinger

SONGS TO KNOW AND SING

31. Which 1969 hit employed 42 vocalists?

    (a) "Stand by Your Man" (Tammy Wynette)

    (b) "Morning Girl" (Neon Philharmonic)

    (c) "Oh Happy Day" (Edwin Hawkins Singers)

    (d) "Israelites" (Desmond Dekker and the Aces)

    (e) "In the Year 2525 (Exordium and Terminus)" (Zager and Evans)

32. Which 1965 single uses the word "no" in the lyrics more than 60 times?

    (a) "Not a Second Time" (Beatles)

    (b) "No Milk Today" (Herman's Hermits)

    (c) "No Particular Place to Go" (Chuck Berry)

    (d) "Not Me" (Orlons)

    (e) "Tell Her No" (Zombies)

33. Which hugely popular 1963 folk song was the subject of controversy over its lyrics, which some took to be about smoking marijuana?

    (a) "Cocaine Blues" (Dave Van Ronk)
    (b) "The Banana Boat Song" (Tarriers)
    (c) "Mister Spaceman" (Holy Modal Rounders)
    (d) "High Flying Bird" (Richie Havens)
    (e) "Puff the Magic Dragon" (Peter, Paul and Mary)

34. In 1967, Mitch Ryder and the Detroit Wheels had a big single titled for a '60s catchphrase. Which was it?

    (a) "Here Come the Judge"
    (b) "Sock It to Me, Baby"
    (c) "You Bet Your Bippy"
    (d) "Watching the Submarine Races"
    (e) "Do Your Own Thing"

35. Which Holland-Dozier-Holland song, originally done in 1966 by the Supremes, became the first smash for Vanilla Fudge two years later?

    (a) "Stop! In the Name of Love"
    (b) "Back in My Arms Again"
    (c) "My World Is Empty Without You"
    (d) "You Can't Hurry Love"
    (e) "You Keep Me Hangin' On"

ROLLING STONES

36. With which song did the Stones first top the American charts?

    (a) "The Last Time"
    (b) "Get Off My Cloud"
    (c) "19th Nervous Breakdown"
    (d) "Under My Thumb"
    (e) "(I Can't Get No) Satisfaction"

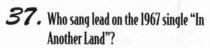

37. Who sang lead on the 1967 single "In Another Land"?

    (a) Brian Jones
    (b) Mick Jagger
    (c) Keith Richards
    (d) Bill Wyman
    (e) Charlie Watts

38. In December 1968, the group staged an event entitled the Rolling Stones Rock and Roll Circus. What was it planned as?

    (a) a party at which musicians and animals performed tricks
    (b) a picnic
    (c) a performance-art happening
    (d) a recording session
    (e) a television broadcast

39. Which member of the Rolling Stones makes an offstage cameo appearance in the documentary film <u>Monterey Pop</u>?

    (a) Brian Jones
    (b) Mick Jagger
    (c) Keith Richards
    (d) Bill Wyman
    (e) Charlie Watts

40. Which label released the Rolling Stones' records in America throughout the 1960s?

    (a) Rolling Stones Records
    (b) London
    (c) Decca
    (d) Atlantic
    (e) Columbia

AGEISM

················

41. Which Beatle was born first?

    (a) John Lennon

    (b) Paul McCartney

    (c) George Harrison

    (d) Ringo Starr

    (e) Pete Best

42. Which of these '60s folk-rockers was born in the 1950s?

    (a) Joan Baez

    (b) Phil Ochs

    (c) Janis Ian

    (d) Melanie

    (e) Mama Cass Elliot

43. Which one of these was born after 1944?

    (a) Bob Dylan

    (b) Jimi Hendrix

    (c) Pete Townshend

    (d) Jerry Garcia

    (e) Aretha Franklin

44. Which Rolling Stone is the oldest?

    (a) Mick Jagger

    (b) Keith Richards

    (c) Charlie Watts

    (d) Bill Wyman

    (e) Ron Wood

45. Which one of these notables turned 50 in 1990?

    (a) Phil Spector

(b) Cher
(c) Chuck Berry
(d) Tina Turner
> (e) Judy Collins

♫ FREESTYLE FINALE
....

46. What former career do singers Rufus Thomas, Sly Stone, Peter Wolf, and the Big Bopper all have in common?

(a) disc jockey
(b) parking lot attendant
(c) office clerk
(d) short-order cook
(e) newspaper reporter

47. Whose photograph was on the cover of the first issue of <u>Rolling Stone</u> magazine in 1967?

(a) Mick Jagger
(b) Dr. Hook
(c) John Lennon
(d) Bob Dylan
(e) Keith Richards

48. What classic rock 'n' roll song first popularized in the early '60s almost became the official state song of Washington in 1985?

(a) "Kicks"
(b) "Apples, Peaches, Pumpkin Pie"
(c) "Rocky Mountain High"
(d) "Louie Louie"
(e) "Little Green Apples"

49. One of rock's most tragic ironies: what vocal duo released a single entitled "Dead

Man's Curve" two years before the California car crash that essentially ended their career?

(a) Jan and Dean

(b) Ian and Sylvia

(c) Everly Brothers

(d) Loggins and Messina

(e) Righteous Brothers

50. Which two of these people are actually related?

(a) B. J. Thomas   (f) Mickey Thomas

(b) Carla Thomas   (g) Nicky Thomas

(c) Earl Thomas   (h) Ray Thomas

(d) Ian Thomas   (i) Rufus Thomas

(e) Irma Thomas   (j) Timmy Thomas

QUIZ 2: PACE MAKERS

This quiz is a bit harder but offers a fighting chance to trivia amateurs, with multiple-choice questions and matchups. The subjects here are group genealogy, songs, album covers, Motown, geography, and dance stances of the '60s.

SINGERS AND PLAYERS

Choosing from this list of artists, name the subjects of the five descriptions below:

Steve Winwood	Stevie Wonder
Jackie DeShannon	Marianne Faithfull
Eric Clapton	Dusty Springfield
Roy Orbison	Mary Hopkin
Felix Cavaliere	Lulu
Buddy Holly	Cilla Black
Dion DiMucci	Johnny Cash
Skeeter Davis	Frankie Valli
Carl Perkins	Waylon Jennings
Neil Diamond	Neil Young

51. The vocal group that backed this singer/songwriter in the late 1950s was named for a street in the Bronx neighborhood where they grew up.

52. This future bandleader and solo star was the 18-year-old vocalist and organist on the Spencer Davis Group's two big numbers, "Gimme Some Lovin'" and "I'm a Man."

53. Besides his own plentiful success, songs by this Texas-born performer—who toured Britain with the Beatles in 1963—became hits for numerous artists, including the Everly Brothers, Don McLean, Linda Ronstadt, and Van Halen.

54. In 1964, this London teenager fresh from a convent school hit the secular charts with "As Tears Go By," a song written for her by the Rolling Stones.

55. This Glasgow lass, who at 15 fronted a roaring R&B band called the Luvvers, made it big singing the titular ballad to a 1967 American movie.

PREVIOUSLY KNOWN AS

For the next five questions, pick out a former name of each group:

56. Who

(a) High Numbers
(b) Tommy and the Bijoux
(c) Action
(d) Shepherd's Bush Mods
(e) Creation

57. Creedence Clearwater Revival

(a) Green River
(b) Golliwogs
(c) Fortunate Sons
(d) Cosmo Boys
(e) Funky Bulldog

58. Alice Cooper

(a) Alan Shepard
(b) Death's Ugly Head
(c) Forensic Scientists
(d) Earwigs
(e) Billion Dollar Babies

59. Led Zeppelin

(a) Honeydrippers
(b) Moon's Balloon
(c) New Yardbirds
(d) Dictators
(e) Deep Purple

60. Kinks

  (a) Ravens
  (b) Crows
  (c) Planets
  (d) Muswell Hillbillies
  (e) Village Green Preservation Society

♫ FAMILY TREES

Four of the groups in each set of five have, at one time or another, included someone who was also a past or future member of the band in question. Your job is to pick out the unrelated band—the one with no direct personnel connection—from each gang of five.

61. Cream

  (a) Delaney and Bonnie
  (b) Air Force
  (c) Led Zeppelin
  (d) Graham Bond Organisation
  (e) Tony Williams Lifetime

62. Byrds

  (a) Crosby, Stills, Nash and Young
  (b) Buffalo Springfield
  (c) Flying Burrito Brothers
  (d) New Christy Minstrels
  (e) International Submarine Band

63. Jefferson Airplane

  (a) Big Brother and the Holding Company
  (b) Moby Grape
  (c) Great Society

(d) SVT

(e) Hot Tuna

64. Yardbirds

(a) Illusion

(b) Armageddon

(c) Beck, Bogert and Appice

(d) Pretty Things

(e) Renaissance

65. Move

(a) Mike Sheridan and the Nightriders

(b) Idle Race

(c) Zombies

(d) Electric Light Orchestra

(e) Wizzard

♫ ROOTS, NAMES, AND BRANCHES

The five '60s groups of the next five questions may not exactly be household names, but each was a forerunner–or at least a family tree branch–of a better-known '70s band contained in the accompanying lists.

66. Crazy World of Arthur Brown

(a) Emerson, Lake and Palmer

(b) Hawkwind

(c) Jethro Tull

(d) Judas Priest

(e) ZZ Top

67. John's Children

(a) Devo
(b) Slade
(c) Sparks
(d) Sweet
(e) T. Rex

68. Hourglass

(a) Allman Brothers Band
(b) Doobie Brothers
(c) Nazz
(d) Styx
(e) Time

69. Fuse

(a) Cheap Trick
(b) Chicago
(c) Golden Earring
(d) Mountain
(e) REO Speedwagon

70. Vagrants

(a) Grand Funk Railroad
(b) Humble Pie
(c) Jethro Tull
(d) Mountain
(e) Steely Dan

71. Which bands that began their careers in the 1960s were named for:

(a) a horror novelist
(b) a British agricultural inventor of the eighteenth century
(c) a William Burroughs novel
(d) a 1956 John Wayne movie
(e) a Winston Churchill speech

COVER STORIES
....

72. Which Rolling Stones album was originally released with a seemingly three-dimensional photo of the group glued to the front cover?

   (a) Between the Buttons
   (b) Through the Past Darkly
   (c) 12x5
   (d) Their Satanic Majesties Request
   (e) Flowers

73. In what food is Roger Daltrey sitting on the cover of The Who Sell Out?

   (a) baked beans
   (b) whipped cream
   (c) tomato soup
   (d) Jell-O
   (e) eggs

74. Who drew the cartoon cover of Big Brother and the Holding Company's Cheap Thrills?

   (a) Robert Williams
   (b) R. Crumb
   (c) Charles Schulz
   (d) George Studdy
   (e) Rick Griffin

75. Who painted the primitivist front cover of the Band's Music from Big Pink?

   (a) Garth Hudson
   (b) Pablo Picasso
   (c) Bob Dylan
   (d) Dr. John
   (e) Grandma Moses

76. Not counting "peel slowly and see," what are the only words that appear on the original cover of the first Velvet Underground album?

      (a) The Velvet Underground and Nico

      (b) Lou Reed and the Velvet Underground

      (c) Andy Warhol Presents the Velvet Underground and Nico

      (d) Andy Warhol

      (e) Featuring the underground hit, "Venus in Furs"

IN THE YEAR OF OUR RECORD . . .

77. In which year (between 1960 and 1969) were the following sets of albums released?

      (a) Cheap Thrills (Big Brother and the Holding Company), Wheels of Fire (Cream), Music from Big Pink (The Band)

      (b) Blonde on Blonde (Bob Dylan), Pet Sounds (Beach Boys), The Monkees

      (c) Rubber Soul (Beatles), Highway 61 Revisited (Bob Dylan), Whipped Cream and Other Delights (Herb Alpert and the Tijuana Brass)

      (d) Led Zeppelin, Tommy (Who), Village Green Preservation Society (Kinks)

      (e) Surrealistic Pillow (Jefferson Airplane), Are You Experienced (Jimi Hendrix Experience), Sgt. Pepper's Lonely Hearts Club Band (Beatles)

78. In which year (between 1960 and 1969) were the following sets of singles hits?

      (a) "Duke of Earl," "The Loco-Motion," "Monster Mash," "Telstar"

      (b) "Wild Thing," "Good Lovin'," "You Can't Hurry Love," "Summer in the City"

      (c) "Eve of Destruction," "Hang on Sloopy," "Mr. Tambourine Man," "I Got You Babe"

      (d) "Suspicious Minds," "Dizzy," "Get Back," "Honky Tonk Women"

      (e) "Light My Fire," "Ode to Billy Joe," "Respect," "Daydream Believer"

REMAKE/REMODEL
....

79. All the artists listed under each classic song recorded it. But who among them was the first to release it? (Warning: in some cases, all the bands here were covering someone else's original.)

    (a) "Gloria"
        Doors
        Shadows of Knight
        Patti Smith
        Them

    (b) "Hey Joe"
        Byrds
        Cher
        Jimi Hendrix Experience
        Leaves
        Love
        Wilson Pickett

    (c) "Hang on Sloopy"
        Dino, Desi and Billy
        Jan and Dean
        Ramsey Lewis Trio
        Little Caesar and the Consuls
        McCoys
        Sandpipers
        Vibrations

    (d) "If I Were a Carpenter"
        Johnny Cash and June Carter
        Bobby Darin
        Four Tops
        Leon Russell
        Bob Seger
        Small Faces

    (e) "I Heard It Through the Grapevine"

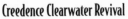

Creedence Clearwater Revival
Marvin Gaye
King Curtis
Gladys Knight and the Pips
Slits
Smokey Robinson and the Miracles

(f) "Stay"
Jackson Browne
Four Seasons
Hollies
Maurice Williams and the Zodiacs

(g) "Good Lovin'"
Dino, Desi and Billy
Olympics
Young Rascals

(h) "Mustang Sally"
Wilson Pickett
Sir Mack Rice
Young Rascals

(i) "Respect"
Aretha Franklin
Rationals
Otis Redding
Vagrants

(j) "Piece of My Heart"
Big Brother and the Holding Company
Erma Franklin

80. And five more, a bit harder this time:

(a) "Take Good Care of My Baby"
Smokie
Bobby Vee
Bobby Vinton

(b) "Land of 1,000 Dances"
   Cannibal and the Headhunters
   Chris Kenner
   Wilson Pickett
   Thee Midniters
   Rufus Thomas
(c) "Summertime Blues"
   Blue Cheer
   T. Rex
   Who
(d) "Younger Girl"
   Critters
   Hondells
   Lovin' Spoonful
(e) "Barbara-Ann"
   Beach Boys
   Regents
   Who

81. Once the Beatles borrowed a song, it frequently became theirs in the public mind. Some of the tunes—like "Roll Over Beethoven" and "Please Mr. Postman"—were substantial pop hits before the Beatles cut them, but once songs got swept into the rush of Beatlemania, misapprehensions about their authorship spread. Which five of these numbers recorded by the Fab Four were actually covers?

(a) "Boys"   (f) "It Won't Be Long"
(b) "Chains"   (g) "This Boy"
(c) "I'll Follow the Sun" (h) "Till There Was You"
(d) "I'm Down"   (i) "Twist and Shout"
(e) "In My Life"   (j) "You've Really Got a Hold on Me"

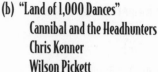

MOTOWN
················

82. What was Motown's slogan?

(a) "Hits from Hitsville"
(b) "All the Hits That Fit"
(c) "Where the Action Is"
(d) "The Sound of Black America"
(e) "The Sound of Young America"

83. All but one of these Motown women sang a hit duet with Marvin Gaye. Which one didn't?

(a) Tammi Terrell
(b) Diana Ross
(c) Mary Wells
(d) Martha Reeves
(e) Kim Weston

84. Which song, co-written by Smokey Robinson and originally intended for the Miracles, instead became the Temptations' first huge hit in 1965?

(a) "Since I Lost My Baby"
(b) "My Girl"
(c) "The Tracks of My Tears"
(d) "Get Ready"
(e) "The Way You Do the Things You Do"

85. How old was Stevie Wonder when he released his first chart-topping single, "Fingertips (Part 2)"?

(a) 10
(b) 11
(c) 12
(d) 13
(e) 14

86. Although he also worked in an automotive factory as a young man, Berry Gordy Jr. had a successful musical career before founding Motown Records. As what?

(a) songwriter
(b) session man
(c) disc jockey
(d) record company executive
(e) art director

LEADERS OF THE PACK

87. Which instrument did these group namesakes play: guitar, bass, drums, or keyboards?

      (a) Dave Clark (Dave Clark 5)
      (b) Ike Turner (Ike and Tina Turner Revue)
      (c) Paul Revere (Paul Revere and the Raiders)
      (d) Manfred Mann (Manfred Mann)
      (e) Buddy Miles (Buddy Miles Express)

88. Which of those five players were also lead singers in their respective groups?

      (a) Dave Clark
      (b) Ike Turner
      (c) Paul Revere
      (d) Manfred Mann
      (e) Buddy Miles

89. Match the singers and their groups:

      (a) Ben E. King   O'Jays
      (b) Levi Stubbs   Righteous Brothers
      (c) David Ruffin   Four Tops
      (d) Eddie Levert   Drifters
      (e) Bill Medley   Temptations

DANCE CRAZY

90. Match the singers to the dance craze they sang about:

Bobby Freeman   Little Eva
Dovells   Dee Dee Sharp
Elvis Presley   Vibrations
Capitols   Jimmy McCracklin
Chubby Checker   Rufus Thomas

(a) Loco-Motion   (f) Watusi
(b) Twist   (g) Mashed Potato
(c) Cool Jerk   (h) Clam
(d) Walk   (i) Bristol Stomp
(e) Funky Chicken   (j) Swim

91. Match the song and the artist most closely identified with it:

(a) "Dance Dance Dance"   Drifters
(b) "Let Her Dance"   Martha and the Vandellas
(c) "Keep on Dancing"   Duane Eddy
(d) "Let's Dance"   Beach Boys
(e) "Save the Last Dance for Me"   Miracles
(f) "Dancing in the Street"   Chubby Checker
(g) "Dance to the Music"   Gentrys
(h) "Dance with the Guitar Man"   Bobby Fuller Four
(i) "Dance the Mess Around"   Chris Montez
(j) "I Gotta Dance to Keep from Crying" Sly and the Family Stone

92. Although "Land of 1,000 Dances" doesn't cite quite as many moves as its title promises, the song does name a lot of steps. Can you come up with five of the seven actually mentioned in the lyrics, as sung by Cannibal and the Headhunters?

93. "Let's Dance" mentions exactly three dances. Name them.

GEOGRAPHY

94. Using the list of cities at the right, from where do these American artists originally hail?

(a)	Chuck Berry	Albany, Georgia
(b)	Bob Dylan	Chicago, Illinois
(c)	Curtis Mayfield	Detroit, Michigan
(d)	Aretha Franklin	Newark, New Jersey
(e)	Chubby Checker	St. Louis, Missouri
(f)	Lesley Gore	Philadelphia, Pennsylvania
(g)	Fats Domino	Englewood, New Jersey
(h)	Lou Reed	Hibbing, Minnesota
(i)	Ray Charles	New Orleans, Louisiana
(j)	Frankie Valli	Brooklyn, New York

95. Not every British group of the 1960s came from London or Liverpool. Which city of the United Kingdom was the hometown of these artists?

(a)	Animals	Andover
(b)	Hollies	Belfast
(c)	Moody Blues	Birmingham
(d)	Them	Blackpool
(e)	Soft Machine	Canterbury
(f)	Joe Cocker	Glasgow
(g)	Donovan	Manchester
(h)	Jethro Tull	Newcastle
(i)	Troggs	Nottingham
(j)	Ten Years After	Sheffield

ODD ACHIEVEMENTS

96. From her majesty's cinematic secret service, which of these vocalists can claim to have sung the title tunes of three James Bond films?

(a) Nancy Sinatra

(b) Barbra Streisand

(c) Matt Monro

(d) Shirley Bassey

(e) Tom Jones

97. Although it sounds enough like a Buddy Holly record to confuse people, 1962's "Sheila" was actually the first hit for:

(a) Tommy Roe

(b) Bobby Hebb

(c) Len Barry

(d) Bob Lind

(e) Brian Hyland

98. Neil Sedaka wrote the million-selling "Oh! Carol" about a New York songwriting friend of his. She composed the thousands-selling "Oh! Neil" as a reply. Who was Carol?

(a) Karen Carpenter

(b) Carole Bayer Sager

(c) Carole King

(d) Carol Kaye

(e) Carol Channing

99. Which singer who had a steady stream of hits from the mid-'50s to the early '60s specialized in bland covers of R&B songs like "Long Tall Sally," "Tutti Frutti," and "Ain't That a Shame"?

(a) Perry Como

(b) Louis Prima

(c) Patti Page

(d) Rick Nelson

(e) Pat Boone

100. Everyone knows that Pete Best was the Beatles' drummer until Ringo Starr replaced him in 1962. But prior to that event, there was another major personnel change in the group. Which bass-playing Beatle left the quintet in 1961?

(a) Rory Storme

(b) Stu Sutcliffe

(c) Klaus Voorman

(d) Tony Sheridan

(e) Frank Ifield

QUIZ 3:
KEEP ON PUSHIN'

If you've gotten this far, you must be ready for a challenge. This section, with only a few multiple-choice questions for the guessers in the crowd, tests your knowledge of the British Invasion, rock politics, music television (pre-MTV of course), and some confusing bits of music lore and lyric you may (or may not) need unconfusing about.

THE BRITISH INVASION

101. Prior to backing Paul McCartney in Wings, Denny Laine was the guitarist/vocalist in another group; he sang lead on that band's 1965 international smash. What group was it?

102. Of the Applejacks, Springfields, Honeycombs, Silkie, Seekers, and Searchers, which group did not contain any female members?

103. The original singer of Manfred Mann, the voice on such hits as "Do Wah Diddy Diddy" and "5-4-3-2-1," also starred in <u>Privilege</u>, the presciently futuristic 1967 film about rock idolatry. Who is he?

104. Although considered part of the British boom, this band—with family ties to AC/DC—came together in Australia with a lineup that was three parts Scottish and two parts Dutch. Who?

105. They enjoyed enormous British success as a singles band—"Sha La La La Lee," "All or Nothing," "My Mind's Eye," and "Tin Soldier" were only some of their big U.K. hits—but this London quartet reached the American Top 40 only once, with a druggy song that introduced a new studio technique to the record world. Who were they?

ILLUSIONS AND CONFUSIONS

106. Besides the hits she recorded under her own name, Darlene Love sang—with or without credit—on tracks by other groups in Phil Spector's stable. Bob B. Soxx and the Blue Jeans often featured her vocals; who was the other main beneficiary of her talents?

   (a) Ike and Tina Turner
   (b) Paris Sisters
   (c) Crystals

(d) Teddy Bears

(e) Ronettes

107. More than a year before Aretha Franklin became a nationwide sensation with "I Never Loved a Man (The Way I Love You)," Fontella Bass released a chart-topping soul classic that sounds strikingly like Aretha's first hits. Name it.

(a) "Rescue Me"

(b) "Since I Fell for You"

(c) "Full Time Woman"

(d) "My Song"

(e) "Reach Out in the Darkness"

108. Although the Ventures are deservedly famous for their twangy instrumentals, they didn't originate 1963's "Wipe Out," the quintessential surf-guitar classic. Which California group did?

(a) Challengers

(b) Chantays

(c) Dick Dale and the Deltones

(d) Hondells

(e) Surfaris

109. There was no person in Lothar and the Hand People named Lothar. Who or what was Lothar?

(a) a drum machine

(b) a Mellotron

(c) a statue

(d) a theremin

(e) a dog

110. Which song that Brian Wilson co-wrote for Jan and Dean, who had a chart-topping hit with it, was never recorded by the Beach Boys?

(a) "Surf City"

(b) "Surfin' Safari"

(c) "Gonna Hustle You"
(d) "Little Old Lady from Pasadena"
(e) "Barbara-Ann"

DOUBLE NEGATIVES

111. Which two of these klassik Kinks singles <u>were not</u> originally released under the band's own name?

(a) "Autumn Almanac"
(b) "Susannah's Still Alive"
(c) "Plastic Man"
(d) "Death of a Clown"
(e) "Sunny Afternoon"
(f) "Everybody's Gonna Be Happy"

112. Which two of the following labels have <u>never</u> had Aretha Franklin on their rosters?

(a) Motown
(b) Atlantic
(c) Columbia
(d) Arista
(e) Stax

113. Which two of the following titles are <u>not</u> Pink Floyd album tracks from the '60s?

(a) "Come in Number 51, Your Time Is Up"
(b) "Several Species of Small Furry Animals Gathered Together in a Cave and Grooving with a Pict"
(c) "Fire Engine Passing with Bells Clanging"
(d) "Gigantic Land-Crabs in Earth Takeover Bid"
(e) "The Nile Song"
(f) "Jugband Blues"

114. Which two of these musicians <u>never</u> worked with Jimi Hendrix, either as employer or employee?
- (a) King Curtis
- (b) Curtis Mayfield
- (c) Curtis Knight
- (d) Billy Cox
- (e) Little Richard
- (f) Miles Davis

115. The Beatles honed their performing skills in Germany and played all over Europe. But in three years of world tours, they didn't reach every corner of the globe. Which two of these nations <u>never</u> witnessed a live Beatles concert?
- (a) New Zealand
- (b) Canada
- (c) Philippines
- (d) Japan
- (e) Korea
- (f) Mexico

THE PARENT TRAP

116. Dino, Desi and Billy had 1965 hits with "I'm a Fool" and "Not the Lovin' Kind." Billy Hinsche was the son of a California real-estate broker. Who were the celebrity fathers of his bandmates in DD&B?

117. The onetime partner of a DD&B parent also sired a rock 'n' roll star. Who is the son and what was the name of his band?

118. Which father and daughter team had a big hit together in 1967?

119. Which '60s folk-rocker has two children who became film actors in the '80s?

120. Who was the first Beatle to become a father?

WASHINGTON
· ·

121. Which soul singer was criticized for performing at Richard Nixon's 1969 inaugural?

122. Which rock 'n' roll singer boasted that Richard Nixon appointed him a federal narcotics agent?

123. Who played the commander-in-chief of the The First Family, a gold-selling 1962 comedy album that spoofed the Kennedy clan?

124. Which not-really-Republican pop group received an invitation from first fan Tricia Nixon and performed at the White House?

125a. Which mid-'60s senator was mimicked in a loopy hit version of "Wild Thing"?

b. Who ostensibly plays the ocarina solo on that record?

SHE COMES IN COLORS
· ·

Supply the phrase missing from each unforgettable opening line.

126. "I see _____ and I want it painted black." ("Paint It Black," Rolling Stones)

127. "All the leaves are brown _____." ("California Dreamin'," Mamas and the Papas)

128. "I, I love the _____." ("Good Vibrations," Beach Boys)

129. "Oh, where have you been _____?" ("A Hard Rain's A-Gonna Fall," Bob Dylan)

MISCONSTRUED LYRICS

Supply the missing, and frequently misunderstood, phrase from these lines:

130. "'Scuse me while I _____." ("Purple Haze," Jimi Hendrix Experience)

131. "You can't raise a Caine back up when _____." ("The Night They Drove Old Dixie Down," the Band)

132. "We skipped the _____." ("A Whiter Shade of Pale," Procol Harum)

133. "_____ will you read my book?" ("Paperback Writer," Beatles)

I FOUGHT THE LAW

134. Who wrote "I Fought the Law"?

135. The legal fur flew when Minneapolis's Trashmen hybridized "Papa-Oom-Mow-Mow" and "The Bird's the Word" to assemble "Surfin' Bird" in 1963. From which Los Angeles vocal quartet did the Trashmen scavenge their source material?

136. Which deejay/concert promoter was investigated in the payola scandals of the early '60s and charged with "commercial bribery"?

137. Which rock 'n' roller spent 18 months behind bars after a Mann Act conviction in 1962?

138. Who recorded hit albums inside Folsom Prison and San Quentin?

TELEVISION

139. What British rock group made its American television debut in June 1964 on The Hollywood Palace, only to be taunted by the show's host, Dean Martin?

140. Which group—besides the Beatles—starred in a Saturday morning cartoon show in the '60s?

141. On The Monkees, it was drummer Mickey Dolenz who sang lead on the opening song, "(Theme from) The Monkees." But on the show's pilot, the track's vocals were by somebody—actually two somebodies—else. Who?

142. Who was the house band on Where the Action Is?

143. Which two of these TV stars did not have an American hit single in the '60s? Shelley Fabares, Richard Chamberlain, Lorne Greene, Debbie Reynolds, Patty Duke, Diana Rigg, Paul Petersen, Sally Field

TIME IS ON MY SIDE

144. In total, how many sides of music comprised the original vinyl editions of All Things Must Pass, Second Winter, Blonde on Blonde, Wheels of Fire, and Woodstock (both volumes)?
- (a) 15
- (b) 18
- (c) 24
- (d) 27
- (e) 30

145. Going by the timing of their original studio album versions, which of these songs runs the longest?

    (a) Rolling Stones: "You Can't Always Get What You Want"
    (b) Beatles: "Hey Jude"
    (c) Bob Dylan: "It's Alright, Ma (I'm Only Bleeding)"
    (d) Doors: "Light My Fire"
    (e) Richard Harris: "MacArthur Park"
    (f) Velvet Underground: "Heroin"
    (g) Crosby, Stills and Nash: "Suite: Judy Blue Eyes"
    (h) Van Morrison: "Cyprus Avenue"
    (i) Vanilla Fudge: "You Keep Me Hanging On"

146. In the heavyweight division (all 10 minutes plus), which of these songs is the longest?

    (a) Bob Dylan: "Desolation Row"
    (b) Doors: "When the Music's Over"
    (c) Creedence Clearwater Revival: "I Heard It Through the Grapevine"
    (d) Chambers Brothers: "Time Has Come Today"
    (e) Rolling Stones: "Goin' Home"
    (f) Mott the Hoople: "Half Moon Bay"
    (g) Neil Young: "Cowgirl in the Sand"

147. Which two of these endless tracks filled an entire album side on their original vinyl releases?

    (a) Grand Funk Railroad: "Inside Looking Out"
    (b) Isaac Hayes: "By the Time I Get to Phoenix"
    (c) Bob Dylan: "Sad Eyed Lady of the Lowlands"
    (d) Iron Butterfly: "In-A-Gadda-Da-Vida"
    (e) Van Morrison: "Madame George"
    (f) Pink Floyd: "A Saucerful of Secrets"
    (g) Jimi Hendrix Experience: "Voodoo Chile"
    (h) Ten Years After: "Help Me"
    (i) Velvet Underground: "Sister Ray"
    (j) Mike Bloomfield/Al Kooper/Steve Stills: "Season of the Witch"

REPLIES

148. What hit single was recorded as a jokey response to "Leader of the Pack"?

149. How did John Lennon answer the reporter's question, posed to him in <u>A Hard Day's Night</u>: "Tell me, how did you find America?"

150. What was Bob Dylan's onstage answer to the heckler who yelled "Judas!" during his performance at London's Royal Albert Hall in May 1966?

MIND BENDERS

QUIZ 4:

OK. This is where the serious fun begins. How's your mental encyclopedia of song lyrics and rock on film? How about release dates and contents of Beatles records? Once you're through those questions, you'll have to rev up the cerebral jukebox to answer queries about such vinyl arcana as instrumentals, novelty records, and B-sides.

♫ BEATLES
....

151. These 10 albums were all released in America between 1963 and 1965. Put them in the correct order of their initial American issue.

> A Hard Day's Night
> The Beatles' Second Album
> Beatles VI
> Beatles '65
> The Early Beatles
> Help!
> Introducing the Beatles
> Meet the Beatles
> Rubber Soul
> Something New

152. The original American editions of <u>Rubber Soul</u> and <u>Revolver</u> contain, respectively, 12 and 11 tracks. The original British albums (as detailed below) each contain 14 songs. Pick out which songs were omitted from the American LPs.

Rubber Soul	Revolver
"Drive My Car"	"Taxman"
"Norwegian Wood"	"Eleanor Rigby"
"You Won't See Me"	"I'm Only Sleeping"
"Nowhere Man"	"Love You To"
"Think for Yourself"	"Here, There and Everywhere"
"The Word"	"Yellow Submarine"
"Michelle"	"She Said She Said"
"What Goes On"	"Good Day Sunshine"
"Girl"	"And Your Bird Can Sing"
"I'm Looking Through You"	"For No One"
"In My Life"	"Doctor Robert"
"Wait"	"I Want to Tell You"

"If I Needed Someone"   "Got to Get You Into My Life"
"Run for Your Life"   "Tomorrow Never Knows"

153. What piece of classical music does John Lennon play on harmonica in <u>Help</u>!?

154. What play from classic English literature turns up in "I Am the Walrus"?

155. Between 1964 and 1973, not counting documentaries, the Beatles—collectively or individually—acted in 10 feature films. Name them.

SONGS AND SONGWRITERS I

156. All these records have one thing in common: the songs were written by famous singers who were not part of the band that had the hit. Who wrote these hits?

   (a) "Woman" (Peter and Gordon)
   (b) "Sit Down, I Think I Love You" (Mojo Men)
   (c) "He's a Rebel" (Crystals)
   (d) "I'm a Believer" (Monkees)
   (e) "San Francisco (Be Sure to Wear Some Flowers in Your Hair)" (Scott McKenzie)

157. Which two of these songs recorded by the Byrds were <u>not</u> written by Bob Dylan?

   (a) "Turn! Turn! Turn!"
   (b) "Paths of Victory"
   (c) "Everybody's Been Burned"
   (d) "You Ain't Going Nowhere"
   (e) "Lay Down Your Weary Tune"
   (f) "Nothing Was Delivered"

158. The Byrds weren't Dylan's only compositional beneficiaries. Manfred Mann, Peter, Paul and Mary, Cher, and the Turtles all did well recording his songs.

Which one of these Dylan tunes <u>wasn't</u> a hit single for any of those four artists?

   (a) "Too Much of Nothing"
   (b) "Don't Think Twice, It's All Right"
   (c) "Mighty Quinn"
   (d) "If Not for You"
   (e) "Blowin' in the Wind"
   (f) "It Ain't Me, Babe"
   (g) "All I Really Want to Do"

159. In 1968, an ex-Yardbird included one of his old band's songs—a number he played on but didn't write—on his first solo album. Who was he and what song did he do for a second time?

♪ SOUL REVIEW

160. "Sweet Soul Music," the 1967 smash by Arthur Conley, pays tribute to a number of soul greats. Which five from this list does he honor?

   (a) Curtis Mayfield
   (b) Otis Redding
   (c) Sam Cooke
   (d) Solomon Burke
   (e) Wilson Pickett
   (f) Lou Rawls
   (g) Percy Sledge
   (h) Jackie Wilson
   (i) Sam & Dave
   (j) James Brown

161. Before becoming a solo star, this Tennessee native played piano on countless sessions and wrote hit songs for Sam and Dave, Johnnie Taylor, Mable John, and others. Who is it?

162a. In 1967, Otis Redding recorded an album with another member of the Stax family. Who was his partner in this one-off project?

b. The first single from their joint LP was a sizable hit and became a soul classic. What song was it?

163a. To which singer—whose name he evidently didn't know at the time—was Elvis Presley paying tribute in these 1956 comments preserved on <u>The Million Dollar Quartet</u> album? "I heard this guy in Las Vegas . . . doing a take-off on me—'Don't Be Cruel.' He tried so hard, he got much better than that record of mine."

b. Name either of the two female singers with whom the subject of Presley's respect recorded duets in the '60s.

164a. Which Beatles song did Ray Charles and Aretha Franklin both cover for chart hits in the late '60s?

b. Which other Lennon/McCartney song was a hit for Ray Charles around the same time?

165. In 1962, as the Valentinos, this band of brothers recorded "Looking for a Love" (later fashioned into a rock hit by the J. Geils Band) and 1964's "It's All Over Now," covered by the Rolling Stones. Valentino wasn't their real family name: what was?

SONGS AND SONGWRITERS II

166. What songs' lyrics include these odd—and not-so-odd—couples?

(a) Julie and Terry

(b) Johnny and Judy

(c) Molly and Desmond

(d) Beethoven and Ma Rainey

(e) The Devil and Carmen

167. Herman's Hermits used material from a diverse collection of songwriters, including Ray Davies ("Dandy") and Donovan ("Museum"). Which American acts did these Hermits hits before Herman?

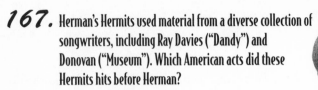

(a) "Wonderful World"
(b) "Silhouettes"
(c) "I'm Into Something Good"

168. Titular inspiration comes from the strangest places. According to its co-author and vocalist, what 1968 frat-rock smash—named for a company sign on a New York building—"would've been called 'Hotel Taft' if I'd been looking in the other direction"?

169. As a tribute to the influential London bands of his youth, David Bowie recorded a dozen favorite songs for his 1973 Pin Ups album. Which eight rock groups originally did these ten Bowie-approved numbers in the '60s?

(a) "I Can't Explain"
(b) "Here Comes the Night"
(c) "See Emily Play"
(d) "Anyway, Anyhow, Anywhere"
(e) "Where Have All the Good Times Gone"
(f) "I Wish You Would"
(g) "Sorrow"
(h) "Rosalyn"
(i) "Don't Bring Me Down"
(j) "Everything's Alright"

ACT NATURALLY
....

170. Name the individual musician or group who had a starring role in each of these films:

    (a) Head (1968)
    (b) Good Times (1967)
    (c) The Fastest Guitar Alive (1966)
    (d) Get Yourself a College Girl (1964)
    (e) Having a Wild Weekend (1965)
    (f) Expresso Bongo (1960)
    (g) Hold On! (1965)
    (h) Tickle Me (1965)
    (i) Girl on a Motorcycle (1968)
    (j) Seaside Swingers (a.k.a. Every Day's a Holiday) (1965)

171. Which noteworthy bands are featured in performance segments of the following movies?

    (a) Blow-Up (1966)
    (b) The Girls on the Beach (1965)
    (c) Bunny Lake Is Missing (1965)
    (d) Here We Go 'Round the Mulberry Bush (1967)
    (e) How to Stuff a Wild Bikini (1965)

172. Who wrote and/or performed the musical scores for these movies?

    (a) More (1969)
    (b) The Family Way (1966)
    (c) Up Tight (1968)
    (d) What's Up Tiger Lily? (1966)
    (e) Poor Cow (1967)

A TRIO OF DOUBLE NEGATIVES

173. Which two of these ten films <u>didn't</u> star Elvis Presley?

(a) <u>Follow That Dream</u>   (f) <u>Easy Come, Easy Go</u>
(b) <u>Flaming Star</u>   (g) <u>Stay Away, Joe</u>
(c) <u>Girl Happy</u>   (h) <u>Spinout</u>
(d) <u>Change of Habit</u>   (i) <u>Speedway</u>
(e) <u>Beat Girl</u>   (j) <u>Speedtrap</u>

174. Which two of these artists were <u>never</u> officially produced by Phil Spector?

(a) Crystals
(b) Ramones
(c) Shangri-Las
(d) Gene Pitney
(e) Bruce Springsteen
(f) Leonard Cohen

175. Which two of these musicians <u>never</u> played bass on a Doors album?

(a) Douglas Lubahn
(b) Larry Taylor
(c) Jerry Scheff
(d) Lonnie Mack
(e) Harvey Brooks
(f) Jack Casady

NOVELTIES

176. What 1969 album, which contains such songs as "I Can't Get No Nookie" and "Saturday Night at the Cow Palace," was reviewed in <u>Rolling Stone</u> before it was even recorded?

177. A comic-book character reached the charts three times in 1966: two versions of an instrumental theme and a song with lyrics. Name the hero.

178. Name any of the three artists involved in question 177.

179. Which two comic-strip characters faced off in a 1966 hit and its 1967 sequel?

180. From which Hollywood musical did the Fifth Estate—a group whose instrumentation included kazoo, electric clarinet, and mandolin—borrow their zany 1967 hit?

181. Which member of Congress was responsible for "Gallant Men," a 1967 chart single?

INSTRUMENTALS

182. In 1962, producer/songwriter Joe Meek launched an instrumental single that became the first American chart-topper by a British rock group. Name the act and its track.

183. The performer purportedly responsible for the 1967 novelty hit "I Was Kaiser Bill's Batman" did not actually participate in the making of the record but was only hired—and given an appropriately descriptive name—as an afterthought. What was that moniker?

184. The T-Bones' 1965 hit "No Matter What Shape (Your Stomach's In)" was actually a cover version of a TV commercial. For what product?

185. The artist who recorded "Music to Watch Girls By," a 1966 instrumental hit later redone (with lyrics) by Andy Williams, is better known for his production and songwriting work with the Four Seasons. Name him.

186. Name all the instrumentals included on the Rolling Stones' first five U.S.

albums (i.e., England's Newest Hitmakers, 12x5, The Rolling Stones, Now!, Out of Our Heads, and December's Children).

ALTER EGOS AND ASSORTED PSEUDONYMS

....

187. Earl Vince and the Valiants, the group credited with 1969's "Somebody's Gonna Get Their Head Kicked in Tonight," was an alias for what well-known British band?

188. What British hit record did Paul McCartney produce under the assumed name Apollo C. Vermouth?

189. Which soon-to-be-huge singer—now a household name—made her pseudonymous recording debut as Bonnie Jo Mason with a 1964 Phil Spector production entitled "Ringo, I Love You"?

190. Under what name was Bob Dylan credited for his contributions to a 1963 recording by Richard Farina and Eric Von Schmidt?

MORE NOMS DE ROCK

....

191. Who was the Wonder Who? and what song? did they cover? for a 1965 hit?

192. The fictitious Nanker Phelge was credited as a composer for which group in its early days?

193. Supply the given names of these performers:

    (a) Sonny Bono
    (b) Ginger Baker
    (c) Fats Domino
    (d) Roger McGuinn
    (e) Syd Barrett

194. What are the real names of these performers?

(a) Chubby Checker
(b) Iggy Pop
(c) Professor Longhair
(d) Captain Beefheart
(e) Bill Wyman

195. Under what stage names are these singers better known?

(a) Frederick Heath
(b) Sharon Myers
(c) Cecil Connor
(d) Charles Westover
(e) Richard Marsh

B-SIDES

196. In 1966, a New York studio engineer named Jerry Samuels released "They're Coming to Take Me Away, Ha-Haaa!" a bizarre and controversial single credited to Napoleon XIV. What was on the 45's B-side?

197. Only one of these Beatles songs—"Day Tripper," "Eleanor Rigby," "Hello Goodbye," "I Saw Her Standing There," "P.S. I Love You," "Rain," and "Strawberry Fields Forever"—was officially an A-side in America. Which one?

198. What was special about the version of "Just Like Tom Thumb's Blues" that appeared on the B-side of Bob Dylan's 1966 single "I Want You"?

199. "Waltz for a Pig," the instrumental flip of the Who's "Substitute," was credited to the Who Orchestra, a pseudonym for another musical outfit entirely. Which group actually recorded the track?

200. Which singer managed to spread a song over two sides of a single at least once a year between 1964 and 1976?

QUIZ 5:

VINYL FINAL

Ready for the real challenge? To make it through this last quiz you'll need only a few things: a head full of '60s lyrics, a knowledge of foreign languages, a complete catalogue of song titles, solid familiarity with musical instruments, and a clear (uh-oh) recollection of Woodstock. Fill up the record (or CD) changer: this one's going to take a while.

SHE

201. To know her is to love her, and to love her is to write songs for her. Each of these lyrics comes from a song that has a woman's name as its title. Name them.

    (a) "You're my pride and joy, et cetera."
    (b) "She's about five-feet-four from her head to the ground."
    (c) "You're so like a woman to me."
    (d) "Who's reaching out to capture a moment?"
    (e) "You were my first love."

202. These may be a little more challenging:

    (a) "I thought we had our love down pat."
    (b) "Her name drives me insane."
    (c) "She is wearing rags and feathers from Salvation Army counters."
    (d) "She moves around like a wayward summer breeze."
    (e) "There's a girl I know who makes me feel so good."

SPEAKING PARTS

What songs include these spoken passages?

203. Easy ones first.

    (a) "Baby, I can't make it without you."
    (b) "I admit you got the biggest brown eyes."

204. These two might be a bit less familiar.

    (a) "As the elders of our time choose to remain blind, let us rejoice and let us sing and dance."
    (b) "Man, that sure is the biggest load of rubbish I ever heard in my life."

205. "He went away and you hung around, and bothered me every night ..." So begins the prelude to "My Boyfriend's Back." But which classic girl-group songs include these spoken lines?

    (a) "He's good bad, but he's not evil."
    (b) "You closed the door to your heart and you turned the key, locked your love away from me."
    (c) "He sort of smiled and kissed me goodbye. The tears were beginning to show."
    (d) "What would you like to be now that you're not a kid anymore?"

206. This one's harder. Name the song in which the following spoken interlude appears: "The sun is shining, the grass is green. The orange and palm trees sway. There's never been such a day in old L. A."

WORDS TO REMEMBER

Identify the person who spoke these immortal(?) words—not part of any song—and the vinyl on which they are preserved.

207. "I think I busted a button on my trousers. I hope they don't fall down. You don't want my trousers to fall down, now do you?"

208. "Four gentlemen and one great, great broad ..."

209. "Is it rolling, Bob?"

210. "I saw ya!"

ESPERANTO

211. Groups occasionally recut their hits in other languages. The Beach Boys sang "In My Room" in German; the Hollies ("Look Through Any Window" became

"Regardez Par des Fenêtres," but it didn't cut the Gallic mustard and was scotched), Elvis Presley, and the Searchers are only some of those who attempted polyglot pop. Supply the familiar English titles of these translated hits:

(a) "Sie Liebt Dich"
(b) "Con Le Mie Lacrime"
(c) "Ragazza Sola, Ragazzo Solo"
(d) "Baby Wo Ist Unsere Liebe"
(e) "Warten und Hoffen"

212. What are the French lyrics that follow "Michelle, ma belle"?

213. What nationality was the Singing Nun (Sister Luc-Gabrielle), the lead voice of 1963's chart-topping smash "Dominique"?

214. What do the old folks say in Chuck Berry's "You Never Can Tell"?

215. In 1963, a foreign song whose original title translated roughly into "Walk with Your Chin Up" (sample lyric: "Sadness hides in the shadows of the stars") sold a million copies in America. In what language was the record?

TWICE UPON A TITLE

Since song titles can't be copyrighted, they can—and occasionally do—appear on different songs. Each of these odd couples shared a song title in the '60s: for instance, the Crazy World of Arthur Brown and the Jimi Hendrix Experience both recorded songs called "Fire"; the Velvet Underground and the Beatles both wondered "What Goes On." It's up to you to figure out what one great thought these pairs of great minds had.

216. Bob Dylan and Canned Heat

217. Velvet Underground and the Who

218. Dave Clark Five and Dave Clark Five

219. Rolling Stones and Aretha Franklin

220. Them and the Beach Boys

GETTIN' MIGHTY SPECIFIC
....

221. By what name is the edifice at 1619 Broadway in New York City also known?

222. Whose address did the Rolling Stones borrow for the title of "2120 South Michigan Avenue"?

223. Name the two American cities mentioned in the lyrics of Martha and the Vandellas' "Dancing in the Street," Chuck Berry's "Back in the USA," and the oft-recorded "Route 66."

224. In what cities are the following song-celebrated places actually located?
- (a) Blue Jay Way
- (b) Goodge Street
- (c) MacArthur Park
- (d) South Street
- (e) Cyprus Avenue

225a. Who sang a musical ode to Salt Lake City?

b. Who named a song after Whittier Boulevard in Los Angeles?

SAN FRANCISCO
....

226. What subsequently famous musician—then serving as A&R man for Autumn Records, where he produced tracks by the Beau Brummels, Mojo Men (a band he fronted for a while), and others—produced the Great Society's solitary single?

227. Predating the do-it-yourself indie rock uprising by nearly a decade, this San Francisco group debuted in 1968 with a self-released mini-album. Name the group and the record.

228. Generally considered the Bay Area's first underground rock band, this influential outfit led by a poster artist began performing in 1965 but didn't get around to releasing an album until 1969. Name the group.

229. Which San Francisco band that began in 1964 included, at one time or another, British session pianist Nicky Hopkins, a future Jefferson Starship vocalist, the author of the Youngbloods' 1967 hit "Get Together," and the more famous guitar-playing brother of Huey Lewis's bassist?

NUGGETS

230. The lyrics to "Dirty Water" include the line "Boston—you're my home" and a mention of the Charles River. From what city did the Standells hail?

231. Roughly a decade before his group, Ram Jam, had its moment of funk-rock fame with the 1977 hit "Black Betty," guitarist Bill Bartlett starred in what Top 40 psychedelic bubblegum ensemble?

232. Which California psych-pop band, which took its name (in part) from a Beatles song, later sent a guitar-playing alumnus to Lynyrd Skynyrd?

233. Along with his two songwriting/production partners, Richard Gottehrer performed in two '60s groups, one of which had a spate of nifty hits in 1965 and '66. The other band is a bit less memorable. Name both.

FESTIVALS

234. At what historic concert event was Bob Dylan openly booed?

235. The Monterey Pop Festival (June 1967) featured 31 acts. Two years later, Woodstock also presented 31 acts. Which nine artists performed at both?

Association
Joan Baez
The Band
Blood, Sweat and Tears
Blues Project
Booker T and the MG's
Buffalo Springfield
Eric Burdon and the Animals
Paul Butterfield Blues Band
Byrds
Canned Heat
Joe Cocker
Country Joe and the Fish
Creedence Clearwater Revival
Crosby, Stills, Nash and Young
Electric Flag
Grateful Dead
Arlo Guthrie
Tim Hardin
Keef Hartley Band
Richie Havens
Jimi Hendrix
Incredible String Band
Jefferson Airplane
Janis Joplin
Al Kooper
Mamas and the Papas

Mar-Keys
Beverly Martyn
Hugh Masekela
Scott McKenzie
Melanie
Steve Miller Band
Moby Grape
Mountain
Laura Nyro
Paupers
Quicksilver Messenger Service
Quill
Lou Rawls
Otis Redding
Johnny Rivers
Santana
John Sebastian
Sha Na Na
Ravi Shankar
Simon and Garfunkel
Sly and the Family Stone
Bert Sommer
Sweetwater
Ten Years After
Who
Johnny Winter

236. Name the bands who opened for the Rolling Stones at Altamont Speedway on December 6, 1969.

ERIC CLAPTON

237. Name all the groups—in order if you can—that had Eric Clapton as a full member during the decade beginning in 1963.

238. Name the first commercially issued song on which Clapton was featured as lead vocalist.

239. Although he played on both of the band's early live albums (Sonny Boy Williamson & the Yardbirds and Five Live Yardbirds) and some assorted studio sides collected on the Crossroads set (among others), Clapton stayed in the Yardbirds long enough to record only three regularly released singles. Name the A-sides.

240. Name all the songs for which Clapton received a full or partial writing credit on Cream's first three albums: Fresh Cream, Disraeli Gears, and Wheels of Fire.

TOOLS OF THE TRADE

241. Over the years, certain big-time musicians have been closely identified with specific instrument brands and models. Name the '60s guitars or basses most associated with the following stars. Commonly used informal names of instruments are allowable.

    (a) Jimi Hendrix
    (b) Brian Jones
    (c) Roger McGuinn

(d) Johnny Winter

(e) Paul McCartney

242. What unique-sounding instrument did Del Shannon's co-writer, Max Crook, play on "Runaway"?

243. Most of the Beatles' music was recorded on two- or four-track tape machines. What was the first Beatles song to be recorded using eight tracks?

COMMON DENOMINATORS

Each of these collections has something in common. Figure out what it is.

244. Gerry and the Pacemakers, Cilla Black, Beatles, Billy J. Kramer and the Dakotas, the Cyrkle.

245. "Sunshine Superman," "I Can't Explain," "You Really Got Me," "Leave My Kitten Alone," "It's Not Unusual."

246. "Not Fade Away," "Willie and the Hand Jive," "Magic Bus," "I Want Candy."

247. Barbarians, Beach Boys, Chuck Berry, James Brown, Marvin Gaye, Gerry and the Pacemakers, Lesley Gore, Jan and Dean, Billy J. Kramer and the Dakotas, Smokey Robinson and the Miracles, Rolling Stones, Supremes.

248. Amboy Dukes, Barron Knights, Count Five, Fleur De Lys, Human Beinz, Merseys, Oscar, Pudding, Rain, the Rovin' Kind.

STUFF NO ONE IN THEIR RIGHT MIND SHOULD REALLY REMEMBER

249. Three members of a British Invasion group credited the authorship of some of their biggest songs to L. Ransford, a name borrowed from a member's grandfather. Which group was it?

250. In 1973, Columbia Records ran a magazine ad for an obscure British album it was reissuing. Adjoining a photograph of New York retailer Bleecker Bob, the ad's tag line read, "At Village Oldies, they get 25 bucks for this album." The group responsible for this "underground classic of the '60s" included Nicky Hopkins, Jon Mark, and Alun Davies. What was it called?

ANSWERS

'60S ROCK HISTORY 101

[10 POINTS PER QUESTION]

1. (a) John Lennon, with typically reckless wit, tweaked the royals at their own party.

2. (d) Bob Dylan was seriously injured in a motorcycle crash near his Woodstock home and spent more than a year out of the public eye.

3. (c) Jim Morrison was arrested on a felony charge of "lewd and lascivious behavior" and three lesser crimes following a Doors concert in Miami in 1969. In September 1970, he was convicted of using profanity and exposing himself; although fined and sentenced to six months of hard labor, Morrison died with the case under appeal.

4. (c) Hair. The musical played off-Broadway, at the Public Theater, for six months before shifting to a "legitimate" venue, the Biltmore, where it spent more than four years. Milos Forman's film of Hair was released in 1979.

5. (e) From $125-a-month business manager of a San Francisco mime troupe, Bill Graham went on to become America's leading rock concert/tour promoter. He died in a 1991 helicopter crash.

THE NAME GAME

[1 POINT PER CORRECT ANSWER]

6. (c) "Five to One"
   (h) "Two Lovers"
   (d) "Quarter to Three"
   (g) "Let the Four Winds Blow"
   (j) "Five O'Clock World"
   (a) "If 6 Was 9"
   (e) "7 and 7 Is"
   (f) "Eight Miles High"
   (b) "Cloud Nine"
   (i) "Ten Little Indians"

[1 POINT PER CORRECT ANSWER]

7. (a) "White Rabbit"
   (b) "Nashville Cats"
   (c) "Tie Me Kangaroo Down, Sport"
   (d) "Pressed Rat and Warthog"
   (e) "I've Got a Tiger by the Tail"
   (f) "A Salty Dog"
   (g) "Little Red Rooster"
   (h) "Pretty Flamingo"
   (i) "Albatross" (not to mention an LP called Penguin)
   (j) "Mickey's Monkey"

[1 POINT PER CORRECT ANSWER]

8. (a) Strawberry Alarm Clock
   (b) Ultimate Spinach
   (c) Lemon Pipers
   (d) Vanilla Fudge
   (e) Peanut Butter Conspiracy
   (f) Chocolate Watch Band
   (g) Electric Prunes
   (h) 1910 Fruitgum Company
   (i) Moby Grape
   (j) Heavy Jelly

[2 POINTS PER CORRECT ANSWER]

9. (a) Vanity Fare
   (b) Tee Set
   (c) Cyrkle
   (d) Frijid Pink
   (e) Spiral Starecase

[2 POINTS PER CORRECT ANSWER]

10. (a) James Brown, the Godfather of Soul, has also been dubbed Soul Brother

Number One, the Hardest Working Man in Show Business, and, briefly in the '70s, the Original Disco Man.

(b) Jerry Lee Lewis is the Killer. No doubt about it.

(c) B. B. King is the King of the Blues. The B. B. moniker was the result of Riley King's 1950s stint on a Memphis radio station, where the singer/guitarist was nicknamed the Beale Street Blues Boy. Nowadays, he owns a music club on Beale Street.

(d) Aretha Franklin—also known as Lady Soul—is the Queen of Soul, the title accorded her 1992 retrospective set.

(e) Eric Clapton was God for a while, back when lead guitarists were thought to practice on Mount Olympus.

MATCHES

[1 POINT PER CORRECT MATCH]

11. (a) Eric Burdon: Animals
    (b) Burton Cummings: Guess Who
    (c) John Fogerty: Creedence Clearwater Revival
    (d) Mark Lindsay: Paul Revere and the Raiders
    (e) Curtis Mayfield: Impressions
    (f) Peter Noone: Herman's Hermits
    (g) Reg Presley: Troggs
    (h) Keith Relf: Yardbirds
    (i) John Sebastian: Lovin' Spoonful
    (j) David Clayton-Thomas: Blood, Sweat and
        Tears

[1 POINT PER CORRECT MATCH]

12. (a) Freddie and the Dreamers
    (b) Tommy James and the Shondells
    (c) Smokey Robinson and the Miracles
    (d) Martha and the Vandellas
    (e) Gerry and the Pacemakers

(f) Sly and the Family Stone
(g) Wayne Fontana and the Mindbenders
(h) Gary Puckett and the Union Gap
(i) Patti LaBelle and the Blue Belles
(j) Mitch Ryder and the Detroit Wheels

[2 POINTS PER CORRECT MATCH]

13. (a) Chad [Stuart] and Jeremy [Clyde]
    (b) Ike and Tina [Turner]
    (c) Jan [Berry] and Dean [Torrence]
    (d) Peter [Asher] and Gordon [Waller]
    (e) Sam [Moore] and Dave [Prater]

[1 POINT PER CORRECT MATCH]

14. (a) Blues Magoos: "(We Ain't Got) Nothin' Yet"
    (b) Count Five: "Psychotic Reaction"
    (c) Every Mothers' Son: "Come on Down to My Boat"
    (d) John Fred and His Playboy Band: "Judy in Disguise (with Glasses)"
    (e) Richard Harris: "MacArthur Park"
    (f) Hombres: "Let It Out (Let It All Hang Out)"
    (g) Bob Lind: "Elusive Butterfly"
    (h) Barry McGuire: "Eve of Destruction"
    (i) Standells: "Dirty Water"
    (j) Mason Williams: "Classical Gas"

[1 POINT PER CORRECT MATCH]

15. (a) Days of Future Passed: Moody Blues
    (b) Electric Ladyland: Jimi Hendrix Experience
    (c) Everybody's in Show-Biz: Kinks
    (d) John Wesley Harding: Bob Dylan
    (e) I Got Dem Ol' Kozmic Blues Again, Mama: Janis Joplin
    (f) Stand!: Sly and the Family Stone
    (g) Surrealistic Pillow: Jefferson Airplane
    (h) We're Only in It for the Money: Mothers of Invention

(i) <u>Wheels of Fire</u>: Cream
    (j) <u>Willy and the Poor Boys</u>: Creedence Clearwater Revival

BEATLES, ROLLING STONES, KINKS, OR THE WHO

[1 POINT PER CORRECT ANSWER]

16. (a) "She's a Woman" Beatles
    (b) "She's a Rainbow" Rolling Stones
    (c) "She's Got Everything" Kinks
    (d) "It's a Boy" Who
    (e) "I'm a Boy" Who
    (f) "Boys" Beatles
    (g) "Wonderboy" Kinks
    (h) "In Another Land" Rolling Stones
    (i) "Rael" Who
    (j) "Shangri La" Kinks

HITS OR MISSES

[2 POINTS PER CORRECT ANSWER]

17. These five actually sold in mass quantities:
    (a) <u>Magic Bus: The Who on Tour</u>
    (d) Cream: <u>Disraeli Gears</u>
    (f) Bob Dylan: <u>Highway 61 Revisited</u>
    (g) <u>Kinks-Size</u>
    (h) Joni Mitchell: <u>Clouds</u>

SUPREMES, SHANGRI-LAS, SHIRELLES, OR THE RONETTES

[1 POINT PER CORRECT ANSWER]

18. (a) "Baby Love" Supremes
    (b) "Be My Baby" Ronettes
    (c) "Baby It's You" Shirelles
    (d) "Baby, I Love You" Ronettes
    (e) "Remember (Walkin' in the Sand)" Shangri-Las
    (f) "Walking in the Rain" Ronettes
    (g) "Dedicated to the One I Love" Shirelles
    (h) "Where Did Our Love Go" Supremes
    (i) "Will You Love Me Tomorrow?" Shirelles
    (j) "Love Is Like an Itching in My Heart" Supremes

AMERICAN OR BRITISH

[1 POINT PER CORRECT ANSWER]

19. (a) Cyrkle: American
    (b) Hollies: British
    (c) Left Banke: American
    (d) Keith: American
    (e) Blues Magoos: American
    (f) Petula Clark: British
    (g) Dusty Springfield: British
    (h) Beau Brummels: American
    (i) Procol Harum: British
    (j) Association: American

DYLAN, DONOVAN, PHIL OCHS, OR THE LOVIN' SPOONFUL

[1 POINT PER CORRECT ANSWER]

20. (a) "Darling Be Home Soon" Lovin' Spoonful
   (b) "Colours" Donovan
   (c) "Tape from California" Phil Ochs
   (d) "To Susan on the West Coast Waiting" Donovan
   (e) "Catch the Wind" Donovan
   (f) "Flower Lady" Phil Ochs
   (g) "Sad-Eyed Lady of the Lowlands" Bob Dylan
   (h) "Do You Believe in Magic" Lovin' Spoonful
   (i) "Ballad of Oxford (Jimmy Meredith)" Phil Ochs
   (j) "Oxford Town" Bob Dylan

ROCKIN' ALL OVER THE GLOBE

[10 POINTS FOR CORRECT ANSWERS TO QUESTIONS 21-24]

21. (b) San Jose

22. (b) Lancashire

23. (e) New Orleans

24. (a) San Francisco

[1 POINT FOR EACH PLACE]

25. (a) "Bristol Stomp"
   (b) "Honolulu Lulu"
   (c) "California Sun"
   (d) "Girl from Ipanema"
   (e) "The Boy from New York City"
   (f) "England Swings"

(g) "Kentucky Woman"
(h) "New York Mining Disaster"
(i) "By the Time I Get to Phoenix"
(j) "Waterloo Sunset"

'60S ROCK HISTORY 102

[10 POINTS EACH]

26. (d) Robert Johnson. Although he was murdered in 1938 and recorded only 29 songs in his entire career, Johnson has been cited by countless blues and rock musicians as a source of inspiration.

27. (e) "Sounds of Silence." Paul Simon and Art Garfunkel had parted company after the unsuccessful release of their first album, Wednesday Morning, 3AM. Unbeknownst to them, their label hired session musicians to electrify the song and rereleased it.

28. (b) Otis Redding. "(Sittin' on) The Dock of the Bay," released shortly after he died in a 1967 plane crash, became the singer's biggest hit.

29. (d) The Nice. Keyboardist Keith Emerson's pioneering classical-rock group contrasted serious music with wild stage antics. The flag-burning incident occurred during a performance of Leonard Bernstein's "America."

30. (e) Badfinger. The song was included in the Magic Christian soundtrack at the end of 1969, although the single didn't chart until the new year.

SONGS TO KNOW AND SING

[10 POINTS EACH]

31. (c) "Oh Happy Day" (Edwin Hawkins Singers)

32. (e) "Tell Her No" (Zombies). "Nobody but Me" by the Human Beinz would beat it

as the decade's most negative single, but too many of its "no"s are uncountably faint in the background, and "nobody" isn't the same as "no."

33. (e) "Puff the Magic Dragon" (Peter, Paul and Mary)

34. (b) "Sock It to Me, Baby"

35. (e) "You Keep Me Hangin' On"

ROLLING STONES

[10 POINTS EACH]

36. (e) "(I Can't Get No) Satisfaction" reached number one in the summer of 1965; "Get Off My Cloud" duplicated the feat that fall.

37. (d) Bill Wyman sang lead on "In Another Land," a song from <u>Their Satanic Majesties Request</u> that flopped as a U.S. single.

38. (e) <u>The Rolling Stones Rock and Roll Circus</u> was filmed—but never broadcast—as a BBC television program. The indoor extravaganza featured the Who, John Lennon and Yoko Ono, Jethro Tull, Eric Clapton, and others.

39. (a) Brian Jones makes a fleeting appearance walking around the festival grounds in <u>Monterey Pop</u>.

40. (b) London . The Stones were subsequently on their own label, first in conjunction with Atlantic, then through Columbia in the '80s. Decca was their first British label.

AGEISM

[10 POINTS EACH]

41. (d) Ringo Starr was born July 7, 1940, three months before John Lennon. Best was born in 1941, McCartney in 1942, and Harrison in 1943.

42. (c) Janis Ian (born May 7, 1951) is the whippersnapper of the bunch. She was just 16 when "Society's Child" made her famous.

43. (c) No need to throw Pete Townshend's indelible words back at him yet again: he was born May 19, 1945. The other four estimable performers listed were born in 1941 or 1942.

44. (d) Recent retiree Bill Wyman, born October 24, 1936 (notwithstanding claims to 1941), is at least five years older than any other Stone. (Ron Wood, the baby of the family, was born in 1947.)

45. (a) Record producer Phil Spector, born Harvey Phillip Spector, turned 50 on December 26, 1990. At decade's end, Chuck Berry was 64, Tina Turner 52, and Judy Collins 51. Born in 1946, Cher is the baby of this gang.

FREESTYLE FINALE

[10 POINTS EACH]

46. (a) Disc jockey. Rufus Thomas spun platters over WDIA in Memphis, Tennessee; Sly Stone deejayed at KSOL and KDIA in northern California. Peter Wolf preceded his singing days in the J. Geils Band as a nonsinging motor-mouth on Boston's WBCN. And the Big Bopper (J. P. Richardson), who sang the 1958 hit "Chantilly Lace" and died in the plane crash that killed Buddy Holly, was an on-air star and program director of KTRM in Texas.

47. (c) John Lennon.

48. (d) "Louie Louie." Paul Revere and the Raiders and the Kingsmen, the two groups that popularized Richard Berry's controversial rock 'n' roll classic in the early '60s, were both from Oregon. Despite the proximity, that doesn't exactly explain why Washington's state government declared April 12, 1985, "Louie Louie Day" and considered (but ultimately rejected) a resolution to make it the state song.

49. (a) Jan and Dean. The pair's 1964 hit concerns a stretch of Sunset Boulevard that runs adjacent to the UCLA campus. In 1966, driving down Sunset a few miles east of that spot, Jan Berry drove his Stingray into a parked garbage truck and sustained major injuries.

50. (b) and (i). Carla Thomas is Rufus Thomas's daughter; both recorded for Stax.

SINGERS AND PLAYERS

[10 POINTS PER CORRECT ANSWER]

51. Dion DiMucci. Dion and the Belmonts, who doo-wopped themselves a string of hits ("A Teenager in Love," "Where or When") between 1958 and 1960, grew up near Belmont Avenue in the Bronx. In 1960, Dion went solo to cut such classics as "Runaround Sue" and "The Wanderer."

52. Steve Winwood. The guitarist/keyboardist was all of 15 when he and his bass-playing brother Muff folded their own group and joined Spencer Davis. In 1966, "Gimme Some Lovin'" and "I'm a Man," both sung and co-written by the precocious teenager, became the Spencer Davis Group's biggest hits.

53. Roy Orbison. The Everly Brothers ("Claudette"), Don McLean ("Crying"), Linda Ronstadt ("Blue Bayou"), and Van Halen ("Oh Pretty Woman") are only some of those artists who've scored with covers of Orbison tunes.

54. Marianne Faithfull. Within a year of convent school, Faithfull had married, met the Rolling Stones, and become a pop star. The Stones later recorded "As Tears Go By" and had a bigger American hit with it than she did.

55. Lulu. The former Marie Lawrie was not yet 16 when she reached the U.K. charts with a frantic rendition of the Isley Brothers' "Shout." Her international break-through came in 1967 when she acted in, and sang the theme song for, <u>To Sir with Love</u>.

PREVIOUSLY KNOWN AS

[5 POINTS PER CORRECT ANSWER]

56. (a) High Numbers. The Shepherd's Bush group was known as the Detours, and then the Who, but the High Numbers was the name on "I'm the Face," their 1964 debut single. The quartet became the Who for good later that year. (Tommy and the Bijoux was a pseudonym Pete Townshend, Ronnie Lane, and Keith Moon used for their appearance on a Mike Heron album.)

57. (b) Golliwogs. Creedence Clearwater Revival was originally known as the Blue Velvets, but when the group began making records in the mid-'60s it was as the Golliwogs. The CCR moniker was adopted in 1967.

58. (d) Earwigs. In Phoenix, Vincent Furnier and his friends used a variety of names, including the Spiders and (demonstrating a certain insect orientation) the Earwigs. They became Alice Cooper upon moving to Los Angeles in 1968. When Alice went solo, three members of the group made a record as Billion Dollar Babies.

59. (c) New Yardbirds. When the Yardbirds broke up in 1968 with a Scandinavian tour left to do, guitarist Jimmy Page recruited a bass-playing friend from his session years, a singer, and a drummer. Billed as the New Yardbirds, the quartet did the tour and two British dates before changing its name to Led Zeppelin.

60. (a) Ravens. Back in Muswell Hill (a north London neighborhood), Dave Davies's band was called the Ravens until his older brother Ray joined it; they renamed themselves the Kinks around the end of 1963.

FAMILY TREES

[10 POINTS EACH]

61. (c) Led Zeppelin. After Cream, Eric Clapton was one of Delaney and Bonnie's Friends; Ginger Baker, who had been in the Graham Bond Organisation with Jack Bruce, formed Air Force. In the early '70s, Bruce delved into fusion jazz with Tony Williams Lifetime.

62. (b) Buffalo Springfield. David Crosby was an original member of the Byrds; ex-Byrds Chris Hillman and Gram Parsons formed the Flying Burrito Brothers; before the Byrds, Gene Clark had been in the New Christy Minstrels, and Parsons had been in the International Submarine Band.

63. (a) Big Brother and the Holding Company. Moby Grape guitarist Skip Spence was the Airplane's original drummer; Grace Slick left the Great Society to join the Airplane. Guitarist Jorma Kaukonen and bassist Jack Casady formed Hot Tuna in the early '70s; Casady later played in SVT, a new wave group.

64.(d) Pretty Things. Following the Yardbirds, singer Keith Relf and drummer Jim McCarty began Renaissance. Relf went on to form Armageddon and, with his sister Jane, the Illusion. Tim Bogert and Carmine Appice had a group with erstwhile Yardbirds guitarist Jeff Beck in the early '70s.

65.(c) Zombies. Roy Wood had been in Mike Sheridan's band before forming the Move; Jeff Lynne joined the Move after fronting the Idle Race. Wood and Lynne created ELO as a Move side project in 1971; Wood exited after one album to assemble Wizzard.

ROOTS, NAMES, AND BRANCHES

[5 POINTS EACH]

66.(a) Emerson, Lake and Palmer. Carl Palmer drummed in the Crazy World of Arthur Brown; he co-founded Atomic Rooster with keyboardist Vincent Crane and then joined up with Keith Emerson and Greg Lake in 1970.

67. (e) T. Rex. Before he was the hippie elf of Tyrannosaurus Rex (which became glam boogie monster T. Rex), Marc Bolan was the teen-dream guitarist of psychedelic provocateurs John's Children, whose 1967 album was entitled Orgasm.

68.(a) Allman Brothers Band. Prior to forming the blues-wailing group that bore their name, Duane and Gregg Allman tried their hands at pop funk, first as the Allman Joys and then, from 1967 through 1968, as the Hourglass.

69.(a) Cheap Trick. In the willfully blurred history of Cheap Trick, Fuse might have been buried were it not for an album the group–which included Rick Nielsen and Tom Peterson, neither in a dominant creative capacity–released on Epic in 1970.

70.(d) Mountain. The Vagrants, led by guitarist Leslie West, released four singles between 1966 and 1968. In the contemporaneous Rock Encyclopedia, author Lillian Roxon described the Vagrants as "the New York sound, hard rock with the currently fashionable psychedelic trimmings."

[5 POINTS PER CORRECT ANSWER]

71. (a) H. P. Lovecraft; the quintet from Chicago even used the writer's words for their

lyrics.
- (b) Jethro Tull
- (c) Soft Machine
- (d) Searchers
- (e) Blood, Sweat and Tears

COVER STORIES

[5 POINTS EACH]

72. (d) <u>Their Satanic Majesties Request</u>

73. (a) baked beans

74. (b) R. Crumb

75. (c) Bob Dylan

76. (d) Andy Warhol

IN THE YEAR OF OUR RECORD

[5 POINTS PER CORRECT YEAR]

77. (a) 1968
- (b) 1966
- (c) 1965
- (d) 1969
- (e) 1967

SINGLES

[5 POINTS PER CORRECT YEAR]

78. (a) 1962
- (b) 1966

(c) 1965

(d) 1969

(e) 1967

REMAKE/REMODEL

[2 POINTS PER CORRECT ANSWER]

79. (a) Them. The Van Morrison composition first appeared as the B-side to a Them single ("Baby Please Don't Go," a sizable U.K. hit) in 1964. Chicago's Shadows of Knight didn't get around to covering "Gloria" until 1966, but their smash version became the one most people know.

(b) Leaves. A '60s garage-band staple, "Hey Joe" was a minor hit for the Leaves (a California group that included future Turtles drummer Jim Pons) in June 1966; the Byrds and Love weighed in with the song later that same summer. Hendrix didn't record it until the beginning of '67.

(c) The Vibrations had a 1964 hit with "My Girl Sloopy," but its co-author, Bert Berns, adjusted the song's title when he gave it to the McCoys, for whom it became a chart-topping hit on Berns's Bang label in 1965.

(d) Bobby Darin. Oregon folksinger Tim Hardin wrote "If I Were a Carpenter" (although he didn't put it on an album until 1967). Bobby Darin, a regular consumer of Hardin songs, released the hit version in 1966. (The Four Tops and Johnny Cash followed suit in '68 and '70.) In an ironic bit of justice(?), the only record Hardin ever took into the charts himself ("Simple Song of Freedom") was written by Bobby Darin.

(e) Gladys Knight and the Pips. Although Marvin Gaye recorded it first, had the bigger hit, _and_ sang the definitive version of Norman Whitfield/Barrett Strong's "I Heard It Through the Grapevine" (critic Dave Marsh named it the "greatest single ever made" in The Heart of Rock and Soul), Gladys Knight's rendition appeared in 1967, a year before Gaye's. Creedence didn't turn their swampy rock mojo on the tune until 1970.

(f) Maurice Williams and the Zodiacs. South Carolina native Williams wrote the oft-covered "Stay" and first sang it with his group on a million-selling single in 1960.

(g) Olympics. "Good Lovin' " had charted for the Olympics, a West Coast R&B

band, nine months before the Young Rascals made it theirs forever in 1966.

(h) Sir Mack Rice. The Detroit singer, a former bandmate of Wilson Pickett's in the Falcons, had an R&B-chart hit with "Mustang Sally" in 1965. The song also appeared as the B-side of the Rascals' "Good Lovin'" months before the far-more-familiar 1966 Pickett smash appeared.

(i) Otis Redding. Otis wrote "Respect" and reached the Top 40 with it in 1965. Aretha Franklin recorded her chart-topping version in 1967. At the Monterey Pop Festival that year, Redding prefaced his performance of it by saying, "A good friend of mine, this girl, just took the song."

(j) Erma Franklin. Janis Joplin learned "Piece of My Heart," a Bert Berns/Jerry Ragovoy composition, from a version Aretha's sister released in 1967.

[5 POINTS PER CORRECT ANSWER]

80.(a) Bobby Vee. Gerry Goffin/Carole King's wistful "Take Good Care of My Baby" was a million-seller for Vee in 1961; Bobby Vinton didn't get around to it until 1968.

(b) Chris Kenner. New Orleans singer Kenner co-wrote "Land of 1,000 Dances" with Fats Domino and recorded it in 1963; it wasn't even his biggest hit ("I Like It Like That" was). Although Wilson Pickett made it into a Top 10 record in 1966, the best-known version (1965) is by Los Angeles's Cannibal and the Headhunters.

(c) Blue Cheer. The inimitable Eddie Cochran co-wrote and recorded "Summertime Blues" in 1958; Blue Cheer supercharged it into the charts a decade later. Although it had been in their live repertoire since at least 1967, the Who didn't 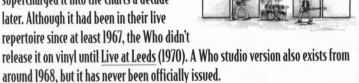 release it on vinyl until Live at Leeds (1970). A Who studio version also exists from around 1968, but it has never been officially issued.

(d) Lovin' Spoonful. John Sebastian and company included his song, "Younger Girl," on a 1965 album; in 1966, New Jersey's Critters named their first album after the song, which became their first (if not biggest) hit.

(e) Regents. Written by a bandmate's brother about their sister, "Barbara-Ann" became the Regents' (a Bronx vocal group of the early '60s) biggest record. The Beach Boys had an enormous hit with the song in early 1966, leading the Who (Keith Moon was a surf-music fanatic) to cover it on an EP that November.

[2 POINTS PER CORRECT ANSWER]

81. (a) "Boys." Luther Dixon and Wes Farrell co-wrote this song for the Shirelles in 1960; although the song wasn't a hit, it was the B-side of "Will You Love Me Tomorrow," which certainly was.

(b) "Chains." Gerry Goffin and Carole King wrote it; the Cookies had the '62 hit with it.

(h) "Till There Was You." This song from The Music Man was written by Meredith Willson. The Beatles weren't even the first act to do a pop cover of it: in 1959 the song provided the dreaded Anita Bryant with her first hit.

(i) "Twist and Shout." Another classic co-written by Bert Berns (under his real surname, Russell), the Isley Brothers rocked this party in 1962.

(j) "You've Really Got a Hold on Me." Smokey Robinson wrote and sang this classic of reluctant romance with the Miracles.

MOTOWN

[5 POINTS PER CORRECT ANSWER]

82. (e) "The Sound of Young America"

83. (d) Martha Reeves

84. (b) "My Girl"

85. (d) 13, although the track was featured on The 12 Year Old Genius album.

86. (a) Songwriter. Gordy co-wrote "Reet Petite," "That's Why," and "Lonely Teardrops," among others, for Jackie Wilson in the late '50s. He also co-wrote the oft-covered "Money."

LEADERS OF THE PACK

[4 POINTS PER CORRECT ANSWER]

87. (a) Dave Clark: drums

(b) Ike Turner: guitar, although he had previously been a pianist.

(c) Paul Revere: keyboards

(d) Manfred Mann: keyboards

(e) Buddy Miles: drums

[10 POINTS]

88.(e) Buddy Miles

[1 POINT PER CORRECT MATCH]

89.(a) Ben E. King: Drifters

(b) Levi Stubbs: Four Tops

(c) David Ruffin: Temptations

(d) Eddie Levert: O'Jays

(e) Bill Medley: Righteous Brothers

DANCE CRAZY

. . . .

[2 POINTS PER CORRECT MATCH]

90.(a) Loco-Motion: Little Eva

(b) Twist: Chubby Checker

(c) Cool Jerk: Capitols

(d) Walk: Jimmy McCracklin

(e) Funky Chicken: Rufus Thomas

(f) Watusi: Vibrations

(g) Mashed Potato: Dee Dee Sharp

(h) Clam: Elvis Presley

(i) Bristol Stomp: Dovells

(j) Swim: Bobby Freeman

[2 POINTS PER CORRECT MATCH]

91. (a) "Dance Dance Dance" Beach Boys

(b) "Let Her Dance" Bobby Fuller Four

(c) "Keep on Dancing" Gentrys

(d) "Let's Dance" Chris Montez

(e) "Save the Last Dance for Me" Drifters

(f) "Dancing in the Street" Martha and the Vandellas

(g) "Dance to the Music" Sly and the Family Stone

(h) "Dance with the Guitar Man" Duane Eddy

(i) "Dance the Mess Around" Chubby Checker

(j) "I Gotta Dance to Keep from Crying" Miracles

[2 POINTS PER CORRECT ANSWER]

92. Pony, Twist, Mashed Potato, Alligator, Watusi, Jerk, Tango

[5 POINTS FOR ALL THREE; NO PARTIAL CREDIT]

93. Twist, Stomp, Mashed Potato

GEOGRAPHY

[1 POINT PER CORRECT MATCH]

94. (a) Chuck Berry: St. Louis

(b) Bob Dylan: Hibbing (he was actually born in Duluth)

(c) Curtis Mayfield: Chicago

(d) Aretha Franklin: Detroit (she was actually born in Memphis)

(e) Chubby Checker: Philadelphia

(f) Lesley Gore: Englewood

(g) Fats Domino: New Orleans

(h) Lou Reed: Brooklyn

(i) Ray Charles: Albany

(j) Frankie Valli: Newark

[2 POINTS PER CORRECT MATCH]

95. (a) Animals: Newcastle

(b) Hollies: Manchester

(c) Moody Blues: Birmingham

(d) Them: Belfast

(e) Soft Machine: Canterbury
(f) Joe Cocker: Sheffield
(g) Donovan: Glasgow
(h) Jethro Tull: Blackpool
(i) Troggs: Andover
(j) Ten Years After: Nottingham

ODD ACHIEVEMENTS

[10 POINTS EACH]

96.(d) Shirley Bassey sang "Goldfinger" (1964), "Diamonds Are Forever" (1971), and "Moonraker" (1979), although only the first was a major American hit for the Welsh vocalist.

97. (a) Tommy Roe

98.(c) Carole King, back when she was still Carole Klein.

99.(e) Pat Boone

100. (b) Stu Sutcliffe was in on the Beatles' five-man formation but bowed out to concentrate on painting, forcing guitarist Paul McCartney to take up bass. Sutcliffe died in 1962 of a brain hemorrhage.

THE BRITISH INVASION

[10 POINTS EACH]

101. Moody Blues. Denny Laine (Brian Hines) was an original member, and he sang the soulful "Go Now!" (a song originally recorded by Bessie Banks). The Moodies didn't develop their classical pretensions until Laine's departure in 1966.

102. Searchers. The Applejacks had a female bassist (Megan Davies); Dusty was one of the Springfields; Honey Lantree was the Honeycombs' drummer (she played the rock'em-sock'em beat on "Have I the Right"); Sylvia Tatler sang in the Silkie (remembered for a wispy 1965 cover of the Beatles' "You've Got to Hide Your Love Away"); and one of the four singing Seekers was Judith Durham.

103. Paul Jones. He also acted in British theater, made solo records, and formed the Blues Band in the late '70s.

104. Easybeats. Dutch guitarist Harry Vanda and Scottish guitarist George Young assembled their group in Australia but moved it to England, where "Friday on My Mind" was a 1966 hit. The two later became a successful writing/production team, working with Marmalade, Flash and the Pan, AC/DC, et al. Malcolm and Angus Young of AC/DC are George's brothers.

105. Small Faces. "Itchycoo Park," the group's only solid U.S. hit (1967), was one of the first records to use the jet-whoosh sound called phasing.

ILLUSIONS AND CONFUSIONS

[10 POINTS EACH]

106. (c) Crystals. Darlene Love, who also sang in the Blossoms, was the vocalist on the Crystals' "He's a Rebel" and "He's Sure the Boy I Love." She also sang Phil Spector hits by Bob B. Soxx and the Blue Jeans ("Zip-a-Dee-Doo-Dah," "Why Do Lovers Break Each Other's Hearts," "Not Too Young to Get Married").

107. (a) "Rescue Me." The song topped the R&B charts in 1965 and was nominated for

a Grammy. The St. Louis singer/pianist was discovered by Ike Turner; she later married and recorded with trumpeter Lester Bowie.

108. (e) Surfaris. The quintet initially released "Wipe Out" as a B-side, but it was flipped when the 1963 single went nationwide. Although "Wipe Out" splashed back into the charts in 1966, the group never had another Top 40 cut.

109. (d) Theremin. Besides providing the Hand People with a gimmick, this early electronic instrument—played by moving hands near an antenna—has cropped up occasionally in rock 'n' roll, used most notably by the Beach Boys on "Good Vibrations" and Jimmy Page onstage.

110. (a) "Surf City" was one of a dozen Jan and Dean songs co-written by Brian Wilson. Both Jan and Dean and the Beach Boys recorded "Little Old Lady from Pasadena" (which Wilson didn't write) and "Surfin' Safari" (which he did, with Mike Love); "Gonna Hustle You" wasn't a Jan and Dean single. Both bands covered "Barbara-Ann"—in fact, Dean Torrence joined Brian to sing the Beach Boys' version.

DOUBLE NEGATIVES

[5 POINTS FOR EACH CORRECT ANSWER, 10 POINTS IF BOTH PARTS ARE CORRECT]

111. (b) "Susannah's Still Alive" and (d) "Death of a Clown" were both issued as Dave Davies singles. The guitarist wrote the songs (the latter with brother Ray) and sang them with the band. Both were substantial U.K. hits in 1967.

112. (a) Motown and (e) Stax

113. (c) "Fire Engine Passing with Bells Clanging" was a Soft Machine track; (d) "Gigantic Land-Crabs in Earth Takeover Bid" was a '70s invention of Hatfield and the North. All the others belong to Pink Floyd.

114. (b) Curtis Mayfield and (f) Miles Davis, although Davis did express serious interest in doing so just prior to Hendrix's death.

115. (e) Korea and (f) Mexico

THE PARENT TRAP

[10 POINTS EACH; NO POINTS FOR HALF-CORRECT ANSWERS]

116. Dean Martin and Desi Arnaz. After the trio disbanded, Hinsche played with the Beach Boys; Dino's sister married Carl Wilson.

117. Gary Lewis (son of Jerry, Dean's longtime comedy teammate) led the Playboys.

118. Frank and Nancy Sinatra scored with "Somethin' Stupid."

119. Donovan (Leitch) is father to Ione Skye (River's Edge, Say Anything) and Donovan Leitch (The Blob, Gas Food Lodging).

120. John Lennon. Cynthia Lennon gave birth to Julian on April 8, 1963. Zak Starkey was born in 1965.

WASHINGTON

[10 POINTS EACH; 5 POINTS FOR EACH HALF OF #125]

121. James Brown. In his autobiography, Brown notes that he had supported Hubert Humphrey in the election, but "it was an honor to be asked to do the gala." By his recollection, he performed "Up Tight" and "Black and Proud." In 1972, Brown endorsed Nixon's reelection campaign and took even more heat for that move.

122. Elvis Presley. What finer irony than a soon-to-be-disgraced law-and-order president bestowing the mantle of drug-law enforcement on a flagrant substance abuser?

123. Vaughn Meader imitated JFK's voice on two albums of Camelot spoofery. His promising comedy career took a nosedive in the fall of 1963.

124. The Turtles. That was in 1969. The following year, Tricia invited Grace Slick to a White House wingding; her date for the evening, Abbie Hoffman, was barred by guards.

125a. Senator Bobby, the "artist" to whom the 1967 single was attributed, was a vocal caricature (by Bill Minkin) of Bobby Kennedy.

125b. The ocarina player was supposedly Ted Kennedy.

SHE COMES IN COLORS

[10 POINTS EACH]

126. "a red door"

127. "and the sky is grey"

128. "colorful clothes she wears"

129. "my blue-eyed son"

MISCONSTRUED LYRICS

[10 POINTS EACH]

130. "kiss the sky"

131. "he's in defeat"—although you wouldn't know it from Joan Baez's lyric-mangling 1971 version

132. "light fandango"

133. "Dear Sir or Madam"

I FOUGHT THE LAW

[10 POINTS EACH]

134. Sonny Curtis. The guitarist for the Crickets—who released their version of the song in 1961—allegedly wrote it in a high school study hall. The Bobby Fuller Four had the hit in 1966, the year Fuller was killed; the Clash revived it in 1979.

135. Rivingtons. According to Al Quaglieri's liner notes for Tube City! The Best of the

Trashmen!, "It starts as a cover of the Rivingtons' 1962 hit, 'Papa-Oom-Mow-Mow.' The wilder, louder, and faster the Trashmen play it, the nutzier the crowds become. The Rivingtons' follow-up, 'The Bird's the Word,' is absorbed into the mayhem, and the medley takes on a life of its own. Local dj/emcee Bill Diehl christens the resulting insanity 'Surfin' Bird.'" The Rivingtons were ultimately awarded composer credit for the Trashmen's secondhand smash.

136. Alan Freed may not have coined the phrase rock 'n' roll, but he certainly did as much as anyone in the '50s to popularize youth music. The congressional investigation of payola snared Freed in 1960; more than two years later, he pleaded guilty and was fined $300.

137. Chuck Berry was convicted of transporting a Texas minor (who turned out to be a prostitute) across state lines and was sentenced to three years in the Federal Medical Center in Springfield, Missouri. He was released in October 1963, having served 18 months.

138. Johnny Cash, who first sang his "Folsom Prison Blues" on a 1956 Sun single, performed for inmates of the California penal institution in 1968 and released a live album of the concert. In 1969, his gig at San Quentin resulted in another million-selling album, this one containing the hit single "A Boy Named Sue."

TELEVISION

[10 POINTS EACH; 5 POINTS FOR EACH NAME IN #143]

139. The Rolling Stones. Dean Martin's comment was "All these singing groups today—you're under the impression they have long hair . . . not true at all, it's an optical illusion. They just have low foreheads and high eyebrows."

140. The Archies.

141. Tommy Boyce and Bobby Hart, the song's writers. Back among the Monkees, Mickey Dolenz also sang lead on "Last Train to Clarksville," "I'm a Believer," "She," "Mary, Mary," and "(I'm Not Your) Steppin' Stone." What was Davy Jones doing all that time?

142. Paul Revere and the Raiders, champions of surreal lip-synching, playing electric guitars and keyboards on the beach.

143. Diana Rigg and Sally Field. The others made their musical names with "Johnny Angel" (Shelley Fabares), "Theme from Dr. Kildare (Three Stars Will Shine Tonight)" (Richard Chamberlain), "Ringo" (Lorne Greene), "Tammy" (Debbie Reynolds), "Don't Just Stand There" (Patty Duke), and "My Dad" (Paul Petersen).

TIME IS ON MY SIDE

[10 POINTS EACH; 5 POINTS FOR EACH CORRECT CHOICE IN #147]

144. (d) 27. All Things Must Pass is a triple-album box; Second Winter, oddly, has three recorded sides; Blonde on Blonde and Wheels of Fire have four each; and the two volumes of the Woodstock soundtrack have a total of 10.

145. (c) Bob Dylan: "It's Alright, Ma (I'm Only Bleeding)." At 7:30, this Bringing It All Back Home number is far from Dylan's longest song, but it tops all the others on the list by at least (in the case of the Stones and CSN) 2 seconds. All the tracks named are about 7 minutes long, with "Cyprus Avenue" and "Light My Fire," at 6:50 each, the most concise.

146. (e) Rolling Stones: "Goin' Home." This 11:35 track, from 1966's Aftermath, was reportedly the first recorded rock song to go to such lengths. After that, however, it was open season on extended workouts. With the exception of Neil Young's relatively brief "Cowgirl in the Sand" (a 10:03 cut on the same LP as the 9:13 "Down by the River"), the songs on this list are all at least 11 minutes long.

147. (c) Bob Dylan: "Sad Eyed Lady of the Lowlands" (although it runs only 11:19, the song fills an entire side of Blonde on Blonde) and (d) Iron Butterfly: "In-A-Gadda-Da-Vida" (the 17:05 side-long centerpiece of the identically titled triple-platinum [!!!] LP).

REPLIES

[10 POINTS EACH]

148. "Leader of the Laundromat," by the Detergents, was a parody of "Leader of the Pack" thrown together by a couple of New York songwriters. Ron Dante (later the voice of the Archies and the Cuff Links) sang it. The record cleaned up, and the Detergents toured, with a gimmick: they threw Salvo tablets (remember them?) at audiences.

149. "Turn left at Greenland."

150. "I don't believe you . . . you're a liar!" According to Paul Cable, in Bob Dylan: His Unreleased Recordings, Dylan then stepped away from the microphone and added "You're a fucking liar" just as the Band (who backed Dylan on that British tour) launched into "Like a Rolling Stone."

BEATLES

[10 POINTS FOR THE CORRECT ANSWER; NO PARTIAL CREDIT]

151. Introducing the Beatles (July 1963), Meet the Beatles (January 1964), The Beatles' Second Album (April 1964), A Hard Day's Night (June 1964), Something New (July 1964), Beatles '65 (December 1964), The Early Beatles (March 1965), Beatles VI (June 1965), Help! (August 1965), Rubber Soul (December 1965).

[2 POINTS FOR EACH CORRECT CHOICE]

152. "Drive My Car," "Nowhere Man," "What Goes On," "If I Needed Someone," "I'm Only Sleeping," "And Your Bird Can Sing," and "Doctor Robert." The reason there are seven, not five, songs is that the American Rubber Soul included two numbers not on the English edition ("I've Just Seen a Face" and "It's Only Love"), and therefore a total of four were deleted from it.

[10 POINTS]

153. The Ode to Joy from Beethoven's Ninth Symphony. With Ringo trapped in the basement of a pub with Roger, the man-eating tiger, John produces a harmonica and joins in the effort to pacify the beast with its favorite piece of music.

[10 POINTS]

154. King Lear. The Beatles' prehistoric sampling effort is detailed by Mark Lewisohn in The Beatles Recording Sessions. The track incorporated "a live feed from a radio..." The tuning dial eventually came to rest on [a BBC production] of Shakespeare's The Tragedy of King Lear. Parts of Act IV Scene VI can be heard on the record....
"Whether the actors concerned... have discovered their appearance on a Beatles record is not known."

[1 POINT PER CORRECT ANSWER]

155. In chronological order, the filmography runs:
A Hard Day's Night (1964)
Help! (1965)
How I Won the War (1967) (John Lennon)

Magical Mystery Tour (1967) (made for British TV but also shown in theaters)
Yellow Submarine (1968) (well, it was their voices . . .)
Candy (1968) (Ringo Starr)
The Magic Christian (1970) (Ringo Starr)
Blindman (1971) (Ringo Starr)
200 Motels (1971) (Ringo Starr)
That'll Be the Day (1973) (Ringo Starr)

SONGS AND SONGWRITERS I

[3 POINTS PER SONG CORRECTLY ATTRIBUTED]

156. (a) Paul McCartney wrote "Woman." Lennon and McCartney also provided Peter and Gordon with "A World Without Love," "Nobody I Know," and "I Don't Want to See You Again."

(b) Stephen Stills wrote "Sit Down, I Think I Love You," a 1967 hit for the Mojo Men. His band, the Buffalo Springfield, also recorded the song.

(c) Gene Pitney. Before amassing a sizable stack of hits as a singer, Pitney penned such venerable rock 'n' roll tunes as "He's a Rebel" and Rick Nelson's "Hello Mary Lou."

(d) Neil Diamond was a staff writer for Don Kirshner when he came up with "I'm a Believer," which turned into the Monkees' second number one single, and its follow-up, "A Little Bit Me, A Little Bit You."

(e) John Phillips of the Mamas and the Papas wrote "San Francisco" for his onetime bandmate (in the Journeymen) Scott McKenzie. Phillips produced and played on the single as well.

[4 POINTS EACH]

157. (a) "Turn! Turn! Turn!" (adapted from the Book of Ecclesiastes by Pete Seeger) and (c) "Everybody's Been Burned" (by David Crosby)

[5 POINTS]

158. (d) "If Not for You." (The New Morning song was, however, a 1971 winner for Olivia Newton-John; George Harrison covered it on All Things Must Pass.) Peter, Paul

and Mary did "Don't Think Twice" and "Blowin' in the Wind" in 1963 and "Too Much of Nothing" in 1967; Manfred Mann did "Mighty Quinn" in 1968. The Turtles had their first hit with "It Ain't Me, Babe," while Cher got hers with "All I Really Want to Do."

[10 POINTS]

159. Jeff Beck. "Shapes of Things," sung by Rod Stewart, is the first song on <u>Truth</u>, Beck's 1968 solo debut. In his droll liner notes, the guitarist suggests the track as "very appropriate background music if you have Vicar over for tea."

SOUL REVIEW

[2 POINTS FOR EACH CORRECT CHOICE]

160. (b) Otis Redding
 (e) Wilson Pickett
 (f) Lou Rawls
 (i) Sam & Dave
 (j) James Brown

[10 POINTS]

161. Isaac Hayes. In the '60s, he co-authored (with David Porter) "Hold On! I'm Comin'," "Soul Man," "You Don't Know Like I Know," "B-A-B-Y," "I Thank You," and others. When Booker T. Jones went off to college, Hayes became a regular member of Stax's house band, playing on countless classic sides. He later became a solo star, topping the charts with "Theme from <u>Shaft</u>" and a stack of gold albums. He also became a producer, an actor, and a record company executive.

[5 POINTS FOR EACH CORRECTLY ANSWERED PART]

162a. Carla Thomas. <u>King & Queen</u>, her album with Otis Redding, reached the Top 40 in 1967.

162b. "Tramp," written by Lowell Fulsom and Jimmy McCracklin.

[5 POINTS]

163a. Jackie Wilson. At the time Elvis saw him, Wilson was singing lead for Billy Ward and the Dominoes.

[5 POINTS FOR EITHER ONE]

163b. Linda Hopkins and LaVern Baker.

[5 POINTS PER CORRECT ANSWER]

164a. "Eleanor Rigby." Ray Charles's version charted in the summer of '68, Aretha Franklin's in the fall of '69.

164b. "Yesterday" was a hit for Ray Charles in late 1967. Quoted by biographer David Ritz, Charles said, "I've never been in love with [the Beatles'] music, but I have liked some of their tunes."

[10 POINTS]

165. Womack. Bobby Womack, who had been a guitar-playing member of Sam Cooke's backup band, led the Valentinos into the mid-'60s and then branched out, doing sessions, songwriting and production for numerous artists (Ray Charles, Joe Tex, Aretha Franklin, et al.) as well as himself.

SONGS AND SONGWRITERS II

[2 POINTS EACH]

166. (a) "Waterloo Sunset" Kinks
   (b) "It's My Party" Lesley Gore
   (c) "Ob-La-Di, Ob-La-Da" Beatles
   (d) "Tombstone Blues" Bob Dylan
   (e) "The Weight" the Band

[5 POINTS]

167. (a) Sam Cooke not only sang "Wonderful World" (1960), he co-wrote the song with Lou Adler and Herb Alpert (under the collective pseudonym Barbara Campbell).

[10 POINTS]

(b) The Rays' version of "Silhouettes" dates back to 1957; the Ronettes had also done the song (1962) before it became a Hermits hit in 1965.

[10 POINTS]

(c) Earl-Jean. Actually, the Cookies singer had an American hit with the Goffin/King composition at the same time (August 1964) Herman's Hermits were having a British chart-topper with the song, which the group learned from a publishing demo. The Hermits' track didn't make it over to the States for a few months, by which time Earl-Jean's hit had faded.

[10 POINTS]

168. "Mony Mony" by Tommy James and the Shondells. In his liner notes to the group's Anthology, Parke Puterbaugh explains that "James had already written and recorded the music . . . but had no words for it. Stuck for a title hours before the vocals were to be laid down, he glanced out the window and saw the name of a major insurance company on an adjacent building: MONY (for Mutual of New York). A lightbulb went off."

[2 POINTS EACH]

169. (a) Who
     (b) Them
     (c) Pink Floyd
     (d) Who
     (e) Kinks
     (f) Yardbirds
     (g) Merseys
     (h) Pretty Things
     (i) Pretty Things
     (j) Mojos

ACT NATURALLY

....

[2 POINTS EACH]

170. (a) Monkees
    (b) Sonny and Cher
    (c) Roy Orbison
    (d) Nancy Sinatra
    (e) Dave Clark Five
    (f) Cliff Richard
    (g) Herman's Hermits
    (h) Elvis Presley
    (i) Marianne Faithfull
    (j) Freddie and the Dreamers

[4 POINTS EACH]

171. (a) The Yardbirds perform "Stroll On" (more or less "The Train Kept a-Rollin' ") in an auto-destruction club scene. The Yardbirds were reportedly Antonioni's second choice after the Who.

(b) The Beach Boys, in their only surf-movie appearance, perform the title track, "Little Honda," and "The Lonely Sea." Brian Wilson, however, was an extra in Muscle Beach Party, and the entire group turned up in The Monkey's Uncle, a Disney flick, singing the theme song with Annette Funicello.

(c) The Zombies make a fleeting appearance on television in this Otto Preminger nerve-wracker, which stars Keir Dullea and Laurence Olivier. As David Ehrenstein and Bill Reed note in Rock on Film, the group "is more prominent in the trailer ... than in the film proper. In the coming attractions, the group holds center stage with sequences never appearing in the final film."

(d) Spencer Davis Group. Traffic (the band Steve Winwood left Davis to form) and Andy Ellison also contributed to the soundtrack of this British comedy but don't appear onscreen. Producer/director Clive Donner, from the album notes: "Never before has the musical score for a film been created the way this one was."

(e) The Kingsmen left Oregon long enough to join in William Asher's fourth Frankie-and-Annette California beach romp, singing the title tune and "Give Her

Lovin','" another timeless pop classic.

[3 POINTS EACH]

172. (a) Pink Floyd
     (b) Paul McCartney
     (c) Booker T and the MG's
     (d) Lovin' Spoonful
     (e) Donovan

A TRIO OF DOUBLE NEGATIVES

[3 POINTS PER CORRECT ANSWER]

173. (e) Beat Girl and (j) Speedtrap

174. (c) Shangri-Las (Shadow Morton was their studio overlord) and (e) Bruce Springsteen, despite the obvious homage of Born to Run's production.

175. (b) Larry "the Mole" Taylor of Canned Heat and (f) Jack Casady of the Jefferson Airplane. All the others on the list were in the bassist-less Doors' bullpen.

NOVELTIES

[5 POINTS]

176. The Masked Marauders. This entertaining boondoggle began with a pseudonymous 1969 review (by Greil Marcus and Bruce Miroff) of a nonexistent supergroup album. ("Dylan's 'Cowpie' is very reminiscent of Billy Ed Wheeler's 'The Interstate Is Coming Through My Outhouse.' . . . This album is more than a way of life; it is life.") A bunch of musical comics promptly cut a record to fit the bill.

[5 POINTS]

177. Batman.

[5 POINTS FOR ANY CORRECT ANSWER]

178. Neil Hefti (who wrote "Batman Theme") and His Orchestra, and the Mar-Kets—a surf twang combo from Balboa, California—each put the TV show's unforgettable dundun-dundun-dundun-dundun riff into the charts as an instrumental. Jan and Dean went so far as to write and record a song called "Batman" and cut a concept album, Jan & Dean Meet Batman. What's more, the Who included the TV tune on their 1966 British EP, Ready Steady Who!

[5 POINTS]

179. Snoopy and the Red Baron. The Royal Guardsmen started off with "Snoopy Vs. the Red Baron," followed it with "The Return of the Red Baron"—using those song titles as the titles of their first two albums—and then rounded off their oeuvre at the end of '67 with "Snoopy's Christmas" and an LP entitled Snoopy and His Friends. In the 1969 words of Lillian Roxon, "Some people question the Royal Guardsmen's imagination."

[5 POINTS]

180. The Wizard of Oz. The Fifth Estate, a Connecticut quintet that started in 1964 and released a fair number of forgotten singles, gave "Ding Dong! The Witch Is Dead" a bizarre rock makeover and got a sizable hit for their trouble.

[10 POINTS]

181. Senator Everett McKinley Dirksen, Republican from Illinois. During the Vietnam War, his recitation of "stories of the American adventure" (accompanied by orchestra) became popular among flag-wavers. The words to this unlikely hit were written by poetic TV newsman Charles Osgood.

INSTRUMENTALS

[5 POINTS]

182. The Tornadoes, "Telstar." Inspired by the American communications satellite, Meek wrote and recorded the song, using a battery-operated keyboard called a

Clavioline for the melody, with a group that had been backing Billy Fury. Released in August '62, the song promptly reached number one in Britain and America, the first record by a British rock group to do so.

[5 POINTS]

183. Whistling Jack Smith was played by Billy Moeller, a Liverpool singer who had nothing to do with the single, a studio concoction. Moeller was engaged to pucker up and blow on the road.

[5 POINTS]

184. Alka-Seltzer.

[5 POINTS]

185. Bob Crewe, who wrote the song "Silhouettes" and produced Mitch Ryder and Lesley Gore as well as the Four Seasons, recorded "Music to Watch Girls By"—a Diet Pepsi jingle—with his orchestra, the Bob Crewe Generation.

[5 POINTS EACH]

186. "Now I've Got a Witness" and "2120 South Michigan Avenue" were included on, respectively, England's Newest Hitmakers and 12x5.

ALTER EGOS & ASSORTED PSEUDONYMS

∙∙∙∙∙∙∙∙∙∙∙∙∙∙∙∙∙∙∙∙∙∙∙∙∙∙∙∙

[10 POINTS PER CORRECT ANSWER]

187. Fleetwood Mac. Written by and featuring guitarist Jeremy Spencer, this greasy retro rock 'n' roll number was the B-side to 1969's "Man of the World."

188. The Bonzo Dog Doo-Dah Band, "I'm the Urban Spaceman." The Bonzos, who appear in Magical Mystery Tour, opened for Cream, and performed at the Isle of Wight Festival, had their sole hit in 1968 with this Neil Innes (later known for his work on the Rutles and numerous Monty Python films) song produced, under a suitably ludicrous moniker, by Paul McCartney.

189. Cher, still a teenager in 1964, had been working for Spector as a backup singer when he let her solo on "Ringo, I Love You," a Beatlemania cash-in (the B-side was "Beatle Blues"). The 45's failure sealed the fate of Bonnie Jo Mason.

190. Blind Boy Grunt. Dylan played harmonica and did some backup vocals on a half-dozen tracks with the two folksingers. Blind Boy Grunt was also the name under which Dylan recorded three of his own songs for a 1963 Broadsides album. Other names used by Dylan for moonlighting: Tedham Porterhouse and Robert Milkwood Thomas.

MORE NOMS DE ROCK

[5 POINTS]

191. Four Seasons, "Don't Think Twice (It's Alright)." The group released two other singles under the not-very-secret pseudonym, but neither was as successful as this 1965 Bob Dylan cover.

[5 POINTS]

192. Rolling Stones. Nanker Phelge (the first name derived from a slang expression Brian Jones used for making horrid faces; the last from onetime Stones roommate Jimmy Phelge) was listed as the author of "Play with Fire" and several other songs.

[2 POINTS EACH]

193. (a) Salvatore
 (b) Peter
 (c) Antoine
 (d) James
 (e) Roger

[3 POINTS EACH]

194. (a) Ernest Evans
 (b) James Jewel Osterberg
 (c) Henry Byrd

(d) Don Van Vliet
(e) William Perks

[4 POINTS EACH]

195. (a) Johnny Kidd
(b) Jackie DeShannon
(c) Gram Parsons
(d) Del Shannon
(e) Sky Saxon

B-SIDES

[10 POINTS PER CORRECT ANSWER]

196. The same track, played backward, with the title "Aaah-Ah Yawa Em Ekat Ot Gnimoc Er-Yeht." Both sides raised the ire of those who found it in questionable taste to make sport of mental illness.

197. "Hello Goodbye." Although both sides of these records all became American hits, the original releases were "We Can Work It Out" b/w "Day Tripper," "Yellow Submarine" b/w "Eleanor Rigby," "I Want to Hold Your Hand" b/w "I Saw Her Standing There," "Love Me Do" b/w "P.S. I Love You," "Paperback Writer" b/w "Rain," and "Penny Lane" b/w "Strawberry Fields Forever." Incidentally, the B-side of "Hello Goodbye" was "I Am the Walrus."

198. Recorded live (in Liverpool), it was Dylan's first commercially available concert recording.

199. Graham Bond Organisation. A legal tussle over the Who song "Circles" (a.k.a. "Instant Party") caused it to be deleted as the British B-side to "Substitute," and a replacement track was needed. Exactly why the organ-playing Bond and his jazzy R&B combo got the job has never been explained; songwriter Harry Butcher is a mystery as well.

200. James Brown. Songs given the two-sided treatment during this period include "Oh Baby, Don't You Weep," "Papa's Got a Brand New Bag," "Say It Loud, I'm Black and I'm Proud," "Mother Popcorn," and "Get Up (I Feel Like Being a) Sex Machine."

SHE

[3 POINTS PER SONG]

201. (a) "Elenore," written and recorded by the Turtles (1968).

(b) "Gloria," written by Van Morrison.

(c) "Carrie-Anne," written by Tony Hicks, Allan Clarke, and Graham Nash and recorded by the Hollies (1967). Continuing the name game, the Hollies also wrote "Jennifer Eccles" and "Dear Eloise" and later covered "Sorry Suzanne" and Bruce Springsteen's "Sandy."

(d) "Windy," written by Ruthann Friedman and recorded by the Association (1967).

(e) "Ronnie," written by Bob Gaudio and Bob Crewe for the Four Seasons (1964).

[5 POINTS PER SONG]

202. (a) "Wendy," written by Brian Wilson and recorded by the Beach Boys (1964).

(b) "Sheila," written and recorded by Tommy Roe (in 1960 <u>and</u> 1962; the second version became the hit).

(c) "Suzanne," written by Leonard Cohen and recorded by Judy Collins (1966) and Noel Harrison (1967).

(d) "Nadine," written and recorded by Chuck Berry (1964).

(e) "Valleri," written by Tommy Boyce/Bobby Hart for the Monkees (1968).

SPEAKING PARTS

[5 POINTS]

203a. "(You're My) Soul and Inspiration," written by Barry Mann and Cynthia Weil and recorded by the Righteous Brothers (1966).

[5 POINTS]

203b. "I Ain't Gonna Eat Out My Heart Anymore," written by Pam Sawyer and Laurie Burton and recorded by the Young Rascals (1965).

[8 POINTS]

204a. "Atlantis," written and recorded by Donovan (1969).

[10 POINTS]

204b. "Story of Bo Diddley," credited to Eric Burdon and Ellas McDaniel and recorded by the Animals (1965).

[5 POINTS PER SONG]

205. (a) "Give Him a Great Big Kiss," written by Shadow Morton and recorded by the Shangri-Las (1965).

(b) "Love Is Here and Now You're Gone," written by Brian Holland, Lamont Dozier, and Eddie Holland and recorded by the Supremes (1967).

(c) "Leader of the Pack," written by Jeff Barry, Ellie Greenwich, and Shadow Morton and recorded by the Shangri-Las (1964).

(d) "Bobby's Girl," written by Henry Hoffman and Gary Klein and recorded by Brooklyn's Marcie Blane (1962). (Susan Maughan had a U.K. hit with the song in 1962; Tracey Ullman brought it around again on her 1983 album.)

[9 POINTS]

206. "White Christmas," written by Irving Berlin and recorded by Darlene Love (1963).

WORDS TO REMEMBER

[5 POINTS]

207. Mick Jagger, playing coy to a Madison Square Garden audience in <u>Get Yer Ya-Ya's Out!</u> Trivia note: the record edits down what Jagger actually said.

[5 POINTS FOR THE NAME, 5 POINTS FOR THE SONG]

208. Bill Graham, introducing Big Brother and the Holding Company in the pseudo-live "Combination of the 2," <u>Cheap Thrills</u>.

[5 POINTS FOR THE NAME, 5 POINTS FOR THE SONG]

209. Bob Dylan to producer Bob Johnston at the start of "To Be Alone with You," Nashville Skyline.

[5 POINTS FOR THE NAME, 5 POINTS FOR THE SONG]

210. Pete Townshend to Keith Moon, who had been trying everyone's patience at a recording session, at the end of "Happy Jack."

ESPERANTO

[5 POINTS PER SONG]

211. (a) "She Loves You," sung in German by the Beatles, who also rendered "I Want to Hold Your Hand" as "Komm, Gib Mir Deine Hand."
    (b) "As Tears Go By," sung in Italian by the Rolling Stones.
    (c) "Space Oddity," sung in Italian by David Bowie.
    (d) "Where Did Our Love Go?" sung in German by the Supremes, who also essayed "Love Is Here and Now You're Gone" in Italian.
    (e) "Wishing and Hoping," sung in German by Dusty Springfield.

[5 POINTS FOR THE EXACT LYRICS—AND SPELLING COUNTS]

212. "... sont les mots qui vont très bien ensemble."

[5 POINTS]

213. Belgian. In The Billboard Book of One-Hit Wonders, author Wayne Jancik recounts the sorry fate of Janine Deckers after her moment of pop glory. "She left the convent ... attempted to continue her singing career and ... recorded a poorly received pro-birth-control tune, 'Glory Be to God for the Golden Pill.' Deckers and her companion of ten years committed suicide in Belgium in 1985."

[5 POINTS]

214. "C'est la vie."

[5 POINTS]

215. Japanese. The song, recorded by Kyu Sakamoto, was retitled "Sukiyaki" for a British instrumental version by Kenny Ball at the end of 1962. Sakamoto's original topped the U.S. singles chart when it was issued in America under that same name in 1963.

TWICE UPON A TITLE

[10 POINTS EACH]

216. "On the Road Again." Dylan sang his song of that name on Bringing It All Back Home (1965); Canned Heat's first hit single (1968) had the same title. Years later, Willie Nelson added another tune to the confusion.

217. "Run Run Run" was (with commas) a Lou Reed song on the first Velvet Underground album (1967) and the first song (no commas) on the Who's Happy Jack LP (1967).

218. "Everybody Knows." The Dave Clark Five recorded two different songs under this title, yielding British hits in 1965 and 1967. The latter, written by Les Reed and Barry Mason, made #2 in the U.K. singles chart.

219. "Think." The Stones' song was included on Aftermath (1966) several months after Chris Farlowe had his first British hit with the Jagger/Richards composition. Aretha Franklin co-wrote and recorded a song under the same name in 1968. James Brown beats 'em all: his first pop hit was the 1960 single "Think."

220. "Here Comes the Night," written by Bert Berns, was Them's second U.K. hit (1965). The Beach Boys' song of the same name, written by Brian Wilson and Mike Love, first appeared on 1967's Wild Honey.

GETTIN' MIGHTY SPECIFIC

[5 POINTS]

221. The Brill Building, early '60s headquarters to such songwriting dynasties as Carole King/Gerry Goffin, Barry Mann/Cynthia Weil, Neil Sedaka/Howard Greenfield, and Doc Pomus/Mort Shuman.

[5 POINTS]

222. Chess Records in Chicago. The Stones recorded at Chess Studios in June 1964, putting down tracks for the 12x5 album, which contains that number.

[5 POINTS FOR EACH CITY]

223. Chicago and Los Angeles.

[1 POINT FOR EACH PART]

224. (a) Los Angeles. In 1967, George Harrison was renting a house on Blue Jay Way, just north of Beverly Hills. He wrote the song there.

(b) London (the Donovan song is entitled "Sunny Goodge Street").

(c) Los Angeles. Jimmy Webb, the song's author, used to go this park on Wilshire and Alvarado.

(d) Philadelphia, as the Orlons sang of their hometown in 1963.

(e) Belfast. Van Morrison's hometown is the site of this monumental song from Astral Weeks.

[5 POINTS]

225a. The Beach Boys did it. Why they did it is another question.

[5 POINTS]

225b. That would be Thee Midniters, a Latin American group from Los Angeles who issued their original lyric-less rave-up in 1965.

SAN FRANCISCO

[5 POINTS EACH]

226. Sylvester Stewart, a.k.a. Sly Stone. The multifarious Texan—musician, disc jockey, talent scout, songwriter, record producer—was working for Autumn Records at the end of 1965 when he was asked to do a session with the Great Society, a San Francisco group fronted by Grace Slick. The resulting single, "Free Advice" b/w "Someone to Love" (later redone by the Jefferson Airplane as "Somebody to Love"— what a difference a syllable makes), was released to little avail in 1966.

227. Flamin' Groovies. Sneakers was a 10-inch released on their own Snazz label. The Groovies—who released a brand-new album in 1992—were signed to Epic and issued their first major-label album, Supersnazz, in 1969.

228. Charlatans. Designer George Hunter sang and Dan Hicks (who later led Dan Hicks and the Hot Licks) played drums in the band's first incarnation, circa 1965. While less intensely boho outfits on the Bay Area underground scene were able to be both hip and commercially viable, the Charlatans' folkie traditionalism doomed them to local legend.

229. Quicksilver Messenger Service. David Freiberg sang and played bass with Quicksilver throughout the '60s; in the '70s he sang with the Jefferson Starship. Quicksilver singer/guitarist Dino Valente wrote "Get Together"; guitarist John Cipollina, later of Copperhead, was the brother of Mario. Hopkins was a member of Quicksilver in 1969.

NUGGETS

[5 POINTS]

230. Los Angeles. The lyrics of this sneering garage-rock classic concern Boston because the song's author, Standells' producer Ed Cobb, wrote it there. When the Inmates, a revivalist British band caught up in the new wave, revived the song in 1979, they customized the lyrics for various American radio markets.

[5 POINTS]

231. Lemon Pipers, who hit it big in 1967 with "Green Tambourine." According to a 1968 issue of Hullabaloo, English-born guitarist Bartlett "has seven pet cats and likes to spend his leisure hours burning holes in his bedspread and smoking cabbage. He is presently a senior in fine arts at Miami University. Favorite things? Ravi Shankar and aluminum foil."

[5 POINTS]

232. Strawberry Alarm Clock. The California group that hit in 1967 with "Incense and Peppermints" picked the first word in its name from the singles charts; lead guitarist Ed King was later in Lynyrd Skynyrd.

[5 POINTS FOR EACH GROUP]

233. Strangeloves, Sheep. In 1965, Gottehrer (future producer of Blondie, the Go-Go's, et al.), Robert Feldman, and Jerry Goldstein decided to try it themselves. They donned wigs and accents, took a name from the Peter Sellers film, and concocted a fib about being three brothers—Miles, Niles, and Giles—from Australia. Their chart hits were "I Want Candy" (later covered by Bow Wow Wow) and "Night Time" (later done by the J. Geils Band). The Sheep, another of the trio's alter egos, released records around the same time.

FESTIVALS

[10 POINTS]

234. The 1965 Newport Folk Festival. Dylan appeared playing an electric guitar, with a backing band of Mike Bloomfield, the Butterfield Blues Band's rhythm section, and pianist Barry Goldberg. While the parochial folk audience heckled, he sang "Maggie's Farm," "Like a Rolling Stone," and "It's All Over Now, Baby Blue."

[2 POINTS FOR EACH GROUP NAMED]

235. Butterfield Blues Band, Canned Heat, Country Joe and the Fish, Grateful Dead, Jimi Hendrix (the Experience did Monterey; at Woodstock, Hendrix was billed as a solo artist), Jefferson Airplane, Janis Joplin (Big Brother and the Holding Company performed at Monterey; she was solo by 1968), Ravi Shankar, and the Who.

[3 POINTS FOR EACH GROUP]

236. Santana, Jefferson Airplane, Flying Burrito Brothers, and Crosby, Stills, Nash and Young (in that order).

ERIC CLAPTON

[1 POINT FOR EACH GROUP; 5 EXTRA POINTS FOR GETTING THEM ALL IN ORDER]

237. Roosters (1963), Casey Jones and the Engineers (1963), Yardbirds (1963–1965), John Mayall's Bluesbreakers (1965–1966), Cream (1966–1968), Blind Faith (1969–1970), Plastic Ono Band (1969), Delaney and Bonnie and Friends (1970), Derek and the Dominos (1970–1971). (Completists may want to add the Powerhouse, a one-off 1966 superstar session, to that list.) After that, excepting guest shots with George Harrison, Howlin' Wolf, and Leon Russell, Clapton went into seclusion; when he returned to active duty in 1974, he was a solo artist.

[10 POINTS FOR THE SONG TITLE; 5 IF ALL YOU KNEW WAS THE ALBUM THAT INCLUDES IT]

238. "Ramblin' on My Mind," a Robert Johnson song included on the 1966 <u>Blues Breakers</u> album by John Mayall with Eric Clapton.

[4 POINTS PER SINGLE]

239. "I Wish You Would," "Good Morning Little School Girl," and "For Your Love." Citing his desire

to stick with the rootsy electric blues on which the Yardbirds had been founded, Clapton objected to the harpsichord pop arrangement of "For Your Love" and left the group on the eve of its release.

[4 POINTS PER SONG]

240. "Strange Brew," "Sunshine of Your Love," and "Tales of Brave Ulysses." All three are on <u>Disraeli Gears</u>. (It doesn't count in this question, but <u>Goodbye Cream</u> contains two more: "Badge" and "Anyone for Tennis.")

TOOLS OF THE TRADE

[3 POINTS FOR EACH INSTRUMENT CORRECTLY NAMED; 1 POINT FOR BRAND ONLY]

241. (a) Fender Stratocaster (he also used a Gibson Flying V on occasion).
    (b) Vox Phantom, commonly known as the Teardrop. (He later switched to a Gibson Firebird.)
    (c) Rickenbacker 12-string.
    (d) Gibson Firebird.
    (e) Hofner Violin bass (which came to be known as a "Beatle bass").

[10 POINTS]

242. Musitron.

[10 POINTS]

243. "Hey Jude." In the summer of 1968, the Beatles took a holiday from their four-track studio home at Abbey Road and recorded this song at Trident Studios, a London facility that had more advanced equipment up and running.

COMMON DENOMINATORS

[5 POINTS]

244. Artists managed by Brian Epstein.

[10 POINTS]

245. Jimmy Page played guitar as a session musician on all these tracks.

[10 POINTS]

246. The "Bo Diddley beat."

[10 POINTS]

247. All these groups appeared in The T.A.M.I. Show film—at least in its original 1965 theatrical version. Shot live onstage in October 1964 at the Santa Monica Civic Auditorium, the "Teenage Awards Music International" film was later reedited to delete the Beach Boys' segment.

[15 POINTS]

248. Bands who covered Pete Townshend songs in the '60s. The roster: Amboy Dukes, "It's Not True"; Barron Knights, "Lazy Fat People" (unreleased by the Who); Count Five, "My Generation" and "Out in the Street"; Fleur De Lys, "Circles"; Human Beinz, "My Generation"; Merseys, "So Sad About Us"; Oscar, "Join My Gang" (unreleased by the Who); Pudding, "Magic Bus"; Rain, "Substitute"; Rovin' Kind, "My Generation."

STUFF NO ONE IN THEIR RIGHT MIND SHOULD REALLY REMEMBER

[10 POINTS EACH]

249. Hollies. Tony Hicks, Allan Clarke, and Graham Nash—the group's songwriters—used that moniker for the credit on most of their early originals.

250. Sweet Thursday. Perhaps the copy wasn't as absurd as Columbia's pseudo-rebellious "The man can't bust our music" campaign, but it did introduce record-collector hype into album advertising. Remember: the more you pay, the better it sounds.